CARAMEL

TRISH DESEINE

CARAMEL

PHOTOGRAPHS BY MARIE-PIERRE MOREL

whitecap

A SMALL MOUTHFUL OF CARAMEL?

Like chocolate, caramel can bring back memories of childhood pleasures. Custards, toffee apples, and candies played a huge part in our celebrations and after-school treats and, as adults, we look back on these pleasures with a sense of comfort.

But there's no need to hark back to the childhood delights of sweet treats as an excuse for enjoying them. It's acceptable to indulge a little nowadays and we should allow ourselves a bit of luxury, without guilt, and without overdoing it!

Caramel is a source of deep satisfaction. It's a marvel to behold in any form—hard, soft, liquid, or frozen—but it's on the palate that the complexity of flavor and texture really comes into its own.

When it's solid and clear it has a pleasing crunch. Golden shards crackle to release the rich flavors of cooked sugar. Mixed with butter and cream, as in soft caramels, it dissolves slowly, sticking to our teeth and forcing our jaws to work harder to fully enjoy the rich flavor.

With cream, as a sauce, as ice cream, or mixed with chocolate, caramel is pure sensuality. The soft and silky texture fills your mouth with pleasure and satisfies from the tip of the tongue to the back of the throat. There's no question of tentatively licking the lips; this needs to be enjoyed by the mouthful!

With a discreet aftertaste that never fails to please, caramel is a welcome addition to a variety of dishes—it brings a note of pleasant sweetness to savory things, adds a finishing touch to cooking juices, and appears on the surface of freshly seared meats and roasted vegetables.

This book offers a wide choice of recipes that are easy to make, without any fussy preparation or need for fancy equipment. Get ready to embark on an easy-going, delightful voyage of discovery through the sensual universe of this unique and magic substance!

HOW IT'S DONE
(HOMEMADE CARAMEL FOR EXPERTS OR CHEATS)

INGREDIENTS

THERE SHOULDN'T BE ANY OILS, CORNSTARCH, OR MARGARINE HERE, NOR ANY OF THE SORTS OF INGREDIENTS THAT CREEP INTO RECIPES FOR CANDY. WHEN PREPARING YOUR CARAMEL, TOFFEE, OR FUDGE, USE ONLY THE BEST-QUALITY SUGAR, BUTTER, AND CREAM AVAILABLE. THESE WILL CERTAINLY NOT BE THE MOST COSTLY ITEMS IN YOUR SHOPPING BASKET AND IT'S WORTH SEEKING OUT THE BEST BASIC INGREDIENTS TO ACHIEVE A DELICIOUS END RESULT.

SUGAR

No matter the form, ordinary white sugar is what's required to make a basic caramel. Until you have mastered the technique, it's always best to add a little water to ensure even distribution of the caramel crystals but, once you're more confident, caramel should be made only from sugar, without any added water.

Darker colored sugars, such as the dry demerara sugar or the moist soft light and dark brown sugars, already have a caramelized flavor. These are worth investigating, or it might be an idea to try the recipe on page 44 for Toffee Sauce made with brown sugar.

BUTTER

The wide range of salted butters on offer makes it possible to add more depth to the salted dimension of caramels. Take care not to overdo it—just a touch of salt is all that's required to enhance the flavor and sweetness.

For those who don't like the sweet–savory alliance, seek out the finest unsalted butter available for a rich flavor. The caramel this butter produces will be greatly enhanced by this attention to detail.

CREAM

My favorite ingredient, as you will probably soon learn, is fresh whipping cream. It's smooth and rich, and the best option for the best result. At a pinch, long-life cream is an acceptable substitute but it always has a sort of "carton" taste and is nowhere near as good as the real thing.

For an even richer and creamier result (at which point all concern for fat intake goes out the window!), I often add some mascarpone, which lends a marvellous velvety texture to caramels. This is best demonstrated in the recipe for Salted Butter Caramel Sauce on page 30, where the full impact of mascarpone comes into its own.

WARNING

This book contains recipes for dishes that are made with raw or lightly cooked eggs. These should be avoided by vulnerable people such as pregnant and nursing mothers, invalids, the elderly, babies, and young children.

EQUIPMENT

SILICONE LINERS

This is the one item of equipment that renders making caramel accessible to all. You can pour golden hot caramel straight onto it, let it cool and/or harden, and lift it off after with no problems. This magical mat is widely available from large supermarkets, kitchenware stores, online retailers, as well as by mail order. There's no excuse for not having one, but even if you don't, you can still make small quantities of caramel using the base of silicone pans.

HEAVY-BOTTOMED SAUCEPAN

When handling dangerously hot caramel, a heavy-bottomed pan is essential to reduce the risk of splashing and it has the added benefit of ensuring even heat distribution. I have several of these pans and the best ones are lined with white enamel, which allows me to gauge the color of the caramel as it goes through its various stages.

Even if I'm only preparing a small amount of caramel, I still use a medium-sized pan. This is because a larger surface makes it easier to monitor the caramelization.

To clean the pans, fill with hot water and let them soak to dissolve the sugar. Even when I've burned the pan and the sugar beyond recognition, when the kitchen is filled with billowing clouds of black smoke, and the caramel looks like bubbling black lava, I've always managed successfully to get the pan clean.

WOODEN SPOONS

There's no need to use anything else. Don't bother with rubber spatulas that will melt in the intense heat, or metal spoons that will conduct the heat to your hands, resulting in burnt fingers and lots of bandages. To be on the safe side, invest in a pair of oven gloves that fit well so that you can grip easily.

CRÈME BRÛLÉE IRON

This is nowhere near as useful as the new, snappy kitchen blow torch, but very useful if the gas canister is empty, or when you feel like a little wistful nostalgia.

PROFESSIONAL KITCHEN TORCH

Forget ovens that can't heat to a high enough temperature, or grill racks that are too high, or too low. This handy little kitchen tool will allow you to create crispy, caramelized shells on the surface of crèmes brûlées, tarts, and pastries. It's extremely easy to use, but naturally I always store it well out of the reach of my children who demonstrate an unhealthy curiosity for pyromania.

PASTRY BRUSH

This is the only utensil that involves a bit of "technique." If you want to obtain a crystal-clear caramel, you must clean the sides of the pan with a damp brush while the sugar is cooking. This immediately dissolves the sugar crystals that form on the sides of the pan and stops them from solidifying the finished caramel.

THE EASY WAY TO MAKE A HARD CARAMEL

THE SCIENTIFIC BIT

Like snow flakes, sugar is a crystal. When it melts the water contained in its molecules renders it liquid. This is why heated sugar dissolves into a syrup. As it boils the water evaporates and the sugar begins to cook and color. Heat breaks up the molecules and transforms the simple taste into a complex mixture of millions of different flavors— all for our pleasure.

This is caramel. The darker it is, the stronger the flavor. But take care—it takes only a few seconds to turn a rich dark caramel into bitter burned sugar.

WITH OR WITHOUT WATER?

Having once seen a professional chef make caramel without using any water, I was eager to do the same. Nowadays, and 200 saucepans later, I can say that I can do it. But it's a precision procedure, so if you're feeling distracted or not too confident, it's always best to add a spoonful of water before starting. This makes the caramel more forgiving and flexible, allowing you more time to get it right, especially if you're using sugar cubes. This only comes into play when making hard caramel for use as a decoration, not for the recipes later on in the book.

If you decide to add water, you'll need to use a specific amount in relation to the weight of sugar used. Allow 1 Tbsp of water for each $1/4$ cup (50 mL) of sugar. One $1/2$ cup less 1 Tbsp (100 mL) sugar will make about 3–4 Tbsp of caramel.

It's best to stir the water into the sugar before you start. It won't dissolve completely and you'll have a sort of thick white paste. Heat the mixture gently to dissolve the sugar completely, then let it boil, brushing down the sides of the pan with a damp brush to remove any crystals that may form. This is a delicate process and, with any luck, you'll succeed in making a clear caramel every time. But sugar loves to crystallize and sometimes you may find you have a thick, crystallized mass that's unusable, and certainly unsuitable for making transparent garnishes.

IT'S BOILING

As soon as the sugar begins to boil you have to watch it carefully. Don't do anything else during these crucial minutes or it'll surely mean disaster. My kitchen ceiling and I know what we're talking about. Caramel begins to form as soon as the sugar comes in contact with the heated sides of the pan. When this occurs, gently turn the pan, altering its position over the flame slightly to evenly distribute the heat source. At this stage, this is the only action you need take. Always be careful not to get burned—remember those oven gloves. Under no circumstances should you stir the caramel or it will crystallize.

After this, it's up to you how dark you want your caramel. From light golden, to amber, to deep mahogany, your caramel will go through a rainbow of hues. It's difficult to judge the taste by the color and, of course, it's too hot to test. Remember that it will continue to cook when removed from the heat, so be wary and, until you are more proficient, err on the side of caution and remove immediately from the heat when you think it's ready.

IT'S COOKED

To stop the caramel cooking, you can put the bottom of the saucepan in a large container of cold water. I prefer simply to wait a bit. The cold-water technique always leaves me with a hard bottom layer and a caramel that hardens quicker than I can use it. However, it takes well to being gently reheated if you need to get it soft again.

And there you have it, over to you to make your liquid gold! It's a fantastic concoction that lends itself to a plethora of creations. This book offers a selection of easy-to-prepare ideas, even for novice cooks.

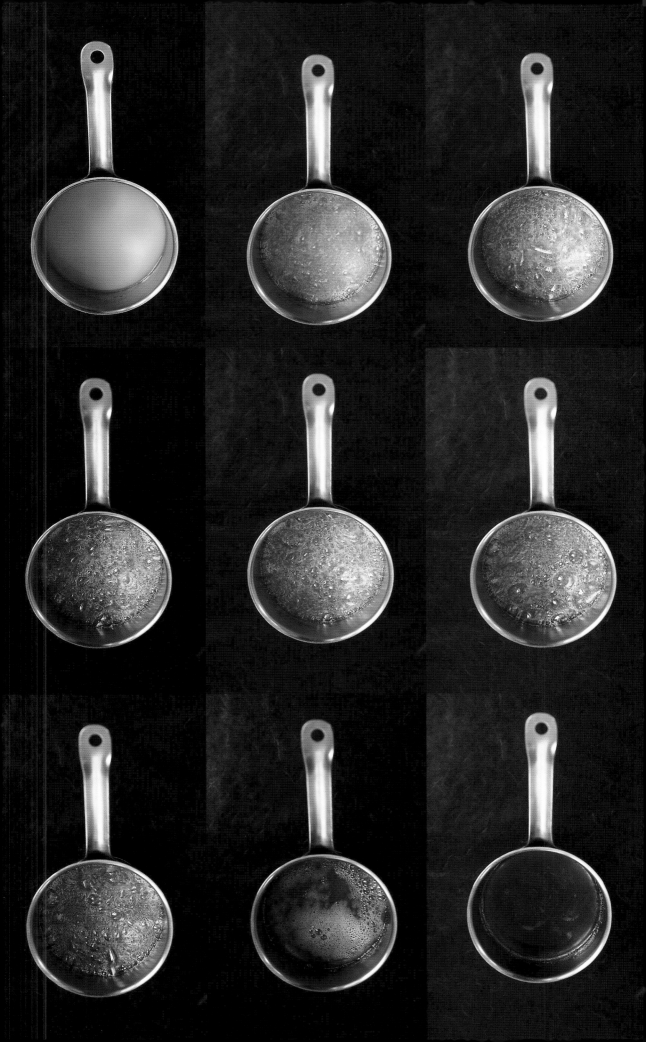

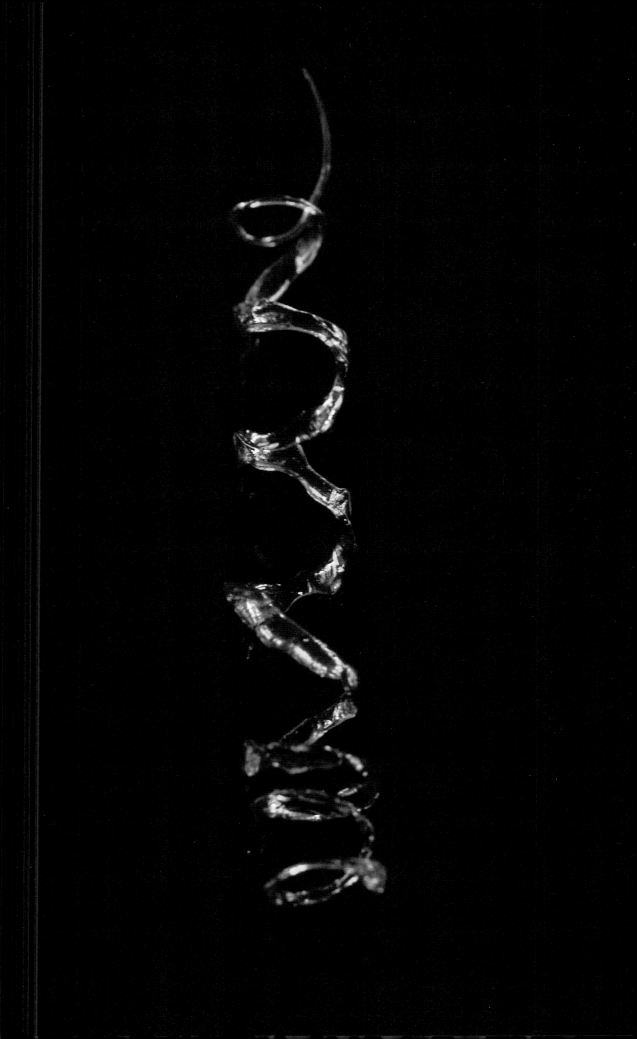

DECORATIONS

TO BE HONEST, IT'S EASIER TO MAKE CARAMEL DECORATIONS WITHOUT A SPECIFIC IDEA IN MIND. DEPENDING ON TEMPERATURE AND FLEXIBILITY, THE CARAMEL WILL BE MORE OR LESS EASY TO MANIPULATE. WHAT'S CERTAIN IS THAT YOUR GARNISHES WILL ALWAYS BE BEAUTIFUL, EVEN IF THEY'RE SLIGHTLY MISSHAPEN OR YOUR CARAMEL'S LESS THAN PERFECT. BE WARY OF MOISTURE AS THIS WILL RUIN YOUR CARAMEL CREATIONS. NEVER PREPARE DECORATIONS TOO FAR IN ADVANCE AND DON'T BE TOO DEMANDING OF PERFECT RESULTS ON A RAINY AFTERNOON. INSTRUCTIONS FOR MAKING THE CARAMEL ARE ON PAGE 12.

SPIRALS

Pour long thin lines of caramel onto a silicone liner. While the caramel is still soft enough to bend, but not so hot as to burn your fingers, twist the strips around the handle of a wooden spoon (try to use a straight one!). Let cool, then remove gently.

NESTS

The proper way to make a caramel nest is to drizzle thin zigzag lines of caramel on the inside of a bowl lined with aluminum foil. Every time I try to do this, my lovely nest breaks when I try to remove it. You may perhaps be more skilled than I am with this technique but my method is to make the same sort of zigzag in a circle on a silicone liner and then, while the caramel is still pliable, draw up the corners of the sheet to form a nest.

CUT-OUT SHAPES

To make the flower shape (pictured top left, opposite), I poured out a small disk of caramel onto the silicone liner. Then, using a nifty Moroccan tool used for making patterns on cookies, I went round the edges while it was still soft to make the pattern.

To use cookie cutters as molds, simply pour the caramel in the middle of the cutter and let it harden before gently pushing the shape out using your thumb.

LOLLIPOPS

Pour out small disks of caramel and then push lollipop sticks in before they harden. You can also add chopped dried fruits, nuts, or even color the caramel with food coloring.

CALLIGRAPHY

Using a small spoon, drizzle out the caramel. Start with individual letters and move on to caramel calligraphy when you're more confident!

PULLED SUGAR

Timing is everything for this procedure because there's a limited time when the sugar is at the correct consistency. Nevertheless, this is caramel at its most spectacular—the results are like golden cotton candy.

The basic technique for achieving pulled sugar is to snip off the ends of a metal whisk, then dip the ends into caramel and drizzle out the thinnest strands possible over a silicone liner.

You can also use a fork, or your fingertips, to pull the strands of caramel before letting them fall onto the liner. This method is slower but you can simply reheat the caramel as necessary.

SHARDS AND GOLD DUST

Caramel is equally dazzling when smashed into thousands of pieces or crushed to a powder!

CARAMEL DIPPED FRUIT

A COATING OF CARAMEL IS USEFUL FOR FRUIT THAT'S FULLY RIPENED—
ANY LONGER AND IT'S ON ITS WAY OUT. TAKE ADVANTAGE AND USE CARAMEL
DIPPED FRUIT TO GARNISH A CAKE OR OTHER DESSERT, OR SERVE AS A
DESSERT IN ITS OWN RIGHT AS A PRETTY ALTERNATIVE TO ORDINARY FRUIT
SALAD. A CRUNCHY COATING THAT REVEALS A JUICY MIDDLE IS A VERY
PLEASING SENSATION.

Choose fresh fruit that's in season, using whole pieces rather than slices.
Strawberries, cherries, and grapes are ideal, as are tangerine segments.
To obtain long thin strands that dangle off the fruit, dip them into the caramel
then pull gently upward out of the pan, allowing the strands to harden.
Cherries are by far the easiest to use; strawberries will need to be skewered
on the end of a skewer or a fork.

CARAMEL DRINKS

THE LATEST TREND IN COFFEE BARS IS A WELCOME INVASION. THERE'S NOW SO MUCH CHOICE ON OFFER: DIFFERENT STRENGTHS, LARGER PORTIONS, VARIETY OF TYPES, FLAVORINGS, AND WHIPPED CREAM TOPPINGS. THE UNITED STATES OFFERS THE WIDEST SELECTION AND EVERY TIME I VISIT, I WANT TO TRY THEM ALL. I SEE EVERYONE ORDERING ALL THE DIFFERENT DRINKS, EACH ONE SEEMINGLY BETTER THAN THE NEXT, BUT WHEN IT'S MY TURN TO ORDER, THE VERY EFFICIENT STAFF ALWAYS PRE-EMPT MY HESITATION AND I INEVITABLY END UP WITH A CARAMEL LATTE.

IT USED TO BE THAT PARISIANS WERE FAR TOO REFINED TO EAT OR DRINK WHILE OUT WALKING, BUT THEY NOW PROUDLY WALK AROUND WITH TAKE-AWAY-CUPS-WITH-A-HOLE-IN-THE-TOP-LID JUST AS COMFORTABLY AS THEIR NEW YORK COUNTERPARTS.

CARAMEL GOES VERY WELL WITH COFFEE AND HOT CHOCOLATE. HERE ARE THREE RECIPES THAT TAKE FULL ADVANTAGE OF THIS DELICIOUS COMBINATION.

HOT MILK CHOCOLATE WITH CARAMEL, WHIPPED CREAM, AND A KICK

TWO HOURS LATER, HAVING HAD TIME TO THINK ABOUT IT, THIS IS WHAT I SHOULD HAVE ORDERED. THE "KICK" COMES FROM THE COFFEE.

1 cup (250 mL) whole milk
$3/4$ cup (175 mL) whipping cream
2 oz (50 g) best-quality milk chocolate
  (alternatively use half milk/half dark chocolate)
Caramel syrup, to taste
1 shot glass or espresso-sized cup of strong espresso coffee

Put the milk and $2/3$ cup (150 mL) of the whipping cream in a saucepan and warm over low heat. Add the chocolate and stir until melted. Stir in the caramel syrup and the coffee. Whip the remaining cream, pour the drink into a mug and top with the whipped cream.

CARAMEL LIQUEUR COFFEE

I use Dooley's for this drink, which is a kind of toffee-flavored Bailey's that I find in the tax free shop at airports. It goes very well with coffee and vanilla ice cream.

Put a scoop of vanilla ice cream in a glass. Pour in some of the liqueur and a shot of strong espresso coffee, to taste.

CARAMEL STIRRING SPOONS

Make a caramel (see page 12) and pour out spoon shapes onto a silicone liner or parchment paper. Let harden and then place in a mug of coffee just before serving. The caramel will dissolve slowly into the coffee.

Alternatively, you can coat the tip of a real spoon with caramel and then dip it into melted chocolate. Or make caramel spoons and dip the tips into melted chocolate.

CARAMEL CHOCOLATE TRUFFLES WITH SALTED BUTTER

Makes about 20 truffles
Preparation time: 20 minutes
Cooking time: 10 minutes
Refrigeration time: 2 hours

1 cup (250 mL) whipping cream
1/2 cup less 1 Tbsp (100 mL) granulated sugar
2 Tbsp (30 mL) salted butter
5 oz (150 g) best-quality dark chocolate,
   broken into pieces
1/4 lb (125 g) best-quality milk chocolate,
broken into pieces
Cocoa powder

Place the cream in a heavy-bottomed saucepan and bring to a boil.

In another heavy-bottomed saucepan, make a caramel from the sugar (see page 12), then remove the pan from the heat and stir in the butter. The mixture will spatter a bit. Immediately stir in the cream and return to the heat to prevent crystals from forming.

Pour the warm caramel cream mixture over the chocolate pieces. Stir until the chocolate has melted and the mixture is smooth.

Chill in the refrigerator, then take pieces of the mixture and form into balls (about marble size) by rolling the mixture between the palms of your hands. Roll the truffles in the cocoa powder. Store in the refrigerator.

CHOCOLATE BUTTERSCOTCH TRUFFLES

Preparation time: 20 minutes
Cooking time: 10 minutes
Refrigeration time: 2 hours

2/3 cup (150 mL) whipping cream
1/2 lb (250 g) best-quality dark chocolate,
   broken into pieces
About 10 butterscotch candies, such as
Werthers Originals

Bring the cream to a boil in a saucepan, then pour over the chocolate pieces. Stir until melted. Let cool sufficiently to handle then take pieces of the mixture and form into balls by rolling between the palms of your hands.

Wrap the butterscotch candies in a tea towel and crush them with a rolling pin.

Roll the truffles in the broken candy pieces. Serve immediately while the caramel is still crunchy.

CARAMELIZED ALMOND AND ORANGE ROCKS

Makes about 20 candies
Preparation time: 10 minutes
Cooking time: 5 minutes

1 cup (110 g) almonds, finely chopped
2 Tbsp (30 mL) corn syrup
5 pieces candied orange peel, finely chopped
1 Tbsp (15 mL) icing (confectioner's) sugar
Dark or milk chocolate, to coat

Preheat the oven to 350°F (180°C).

In a mixing bowl, combine the almonds, corn syrup, and chopped candied orange peel. Drop small mounds of the mixture, spaced well apart, onto a rimmed baking sheet lined with a silicone liner or parchment paper, and dust with the icing sugar.

Place in the center of the preheated oven and bake for 2–3 minutes until golden.

Remove from the oven and let cool completely on a rack. Coat with the melted dark or milk chocolate.

CARAMEL TILES

This is a fantastic way to pair caramel with both unusual and classic flavors. Make a caramel (see page 12). On a silicone liner or parchment paper, arrange small piles of any of the following: popcorn, Rice Krispies, toasted sesame seeds, ground or chopped almonds or hazelnuts. Pour the caramel over each pile and, as it begins to set, flatten them slightly into disks.

Transfer each disk onto a rolling pin to harden into a curved shape, like a roof tile. When they're completely hard, break into irregular shards.

ily
e for . . .

t it all!

© Anne Tainfor

go

SALTED BUTTER CARAMEL SAUCE

THANKS TO THIS RECIPE, YOU'LL HAVE
A LIFETIME SUPPLY OF CARAMEL SAUCE.
ONCE YOU'VE MASTERED THE TECHNIQUE,
YOU WON'T STOP MAKING IT. COLD, THIS
SAUCE CAN BE USED AS A BASE FOR TARTS,
AS A SPREAD, OR AS A DIP. WARM, IT HAS A
VELVETY TEXTURE THAT CAN BE POURED OVER
ICE CREAM, CAKES, OR USED FOR FONDUE.
MASCARPONE COMES INTO ITS OWN AS A
CREAMY BASE, MAKING THIS A REAL TREAT.

Serves 4
Cooking time: 10 minutes

$^1/_2$ cup less 1 Tbsp (100 mL) granulated sugar
2 Tbsp (30 mL) water
$^1/_4$ cup (50 mL) salted butter
1 heaping Tbsp mascarpone

Make a caramel (see page 12) using the sugar and
small amount of water. Remove from the heat and
stir in the butter. The caramel will spatter and
harden in places, but this is normal. Add the
mascarpone and mix in well. Return to the heat
to dissolve any remaining crystals.

Serve the sauce warm or cold.

This sauce will keep in the refrigerator for
4–5 days.

CARAMEL FONDUE

Serves 6–8
Preparation time: 10 minutes
Cooking time: 10 minutes

1 cup (250 mL) granulated sugar
$^1/_4$ cup (50 mL) water
$^1/_2$ cup (125 mL) salted butter
2 heaping Tbsp mascarpone

Follow the instructions for the Salted Butter
Caramel Sauce (left). The quantities are doubled
but the procedure is the same.

Serve the fondue with fresh and dried fruits,
cookies, chocolates—anything that goes well
with caramel and can be skewered on the end
of a fondue fork!

CARAMEL PASTRY CREAM

To fill approx two 9-inch (23-cm) pie crust shells
Preparation time: 10 minutes
Cooking time: 5 minutes

2 x 9-inch (23-cm) ready-to-bake pie crust shells
4 egg yolks
2 Tbsp (30 mL) granulated sugar
1½ Tbsp (20 mL) all-purpose flour, sifted
⅔ cup (150 mL) whipping cream
⅔ cup (150 mL) whole milk
½ cup less 1 Tbsp (100 mL) granulated sugar
2 Tbsp (30 mL) water

Bake the 2 pie crust shells according to the instructions on the package, and set aside to cool.

In a heatproof bowl, beat the egg yolks with the 2 Tbsp of sugar and the flour until light and pale yellow in color, and doubled in volume.

Combine the cream and milk in a saucepan and bring just to a boil.

Make a caramel using the ½ cup less 1 Tbsp sugar and 2 Tbsp of water (see page 12). Remove from the heat and pour in the warm cream mixture. Stir well, then return to the heat to dissolve any crystals that may have formed.

Pour the caramel cream over the egg yolk mixture while stirring vigorously. Return to the saucepan, bring to a boil and simmer for 1 minute, stirring constantly with a wooden spoon until the mixture thickens and coats the back of the spoon.

Let cool completely before spreading in the pre-baked pie crust shells.

CARAMEL FROSTING

To coat 1 large cake or about 2 dozen cupcakes
Preparation time: 10 minutes

2½ cups (625 mL) icing (confectioner's) sugar, sifted
⅓ cup (75 mL) butter, softened
4–5 caramel candies, melted in 4 Tbsp
  warmed whipping cream, then cooled

Put all the ingredients in the bowl of an electric mixer and beat until smooth. Let cool and allow to set slightly before using to frost the cake, so that it doesn't trickle out of control.

CARAMEL CUSTARD SAUCE

Serves 6–8
Preparation time: 10 minutes
Cooking time: 15 minutes

5 egg yolks
⅔ cup (125 mL) granulated sugar
2 Tbsp (30 mL) water
1¼ cups (300 mL) whipping cream
1¼ cups (300 mL) whole milk

Beat the egg yolks with 2 Tbsp of the sugar until light and pale yellow in color, and doubled in volume.

In a heavy-bottomed saucepan, make a caramel with the rest of the sugar and the 2 Tbsp of water (see page 12). Remove from the heat and add the cream and milk. Return to the heat to dissolve any crystals that may have formed.

Pour the caramel cream over the egg yolk mixture, whisking constantly. Pour back into the saucepan and cook, stirring constantly with a wooden spoon, until the mixture thickens and can coat the back of the spoon. Remove from the heat and cool completely before serving.

The same shortcut that applies to ice cream applies here: you can use store-bought caramel sauce to flavor the custard sauce, or use a ready-made custard sauce found in specialty stores and add a caramel flavoring to taste, if you're short on time.

PRALINE

PRALINE IS MADE FROM CARAMEL-COATED
TOASTED ALMONDS OR HAZELNUTS THAT
HAVE BEEN CRUSHED. THE FINER THEY'RE
CRUSHED, THE MOISTER THE MIXTURE
BECOMES BECAUSE MORE OIL IS RELEASED
FROM THE NUTS, MAKING IT ALMOST PASTE-
LIKE IN CONSISTENCY AND A FABULOUS
INGREDIENT FOR DESSERTS AND PASTRIES.

HOMEMADE PRALINE

Cooking time: 10 minutes

$1/2$ cup (75 g) blanched whole almonds or hazelnuts
$1/2$ cup less 1 Tbsp (100 mL) granulated sugar
2 Tbsp (30 mL) water

Lightly toast the almonds or hazelnuts in a dry
skillet. Transfer to a silicone liner to cool.

Make a caramel with the sugar and water (see
page 12). As soon as it turns golden, pour it over
the toasted nuts and let harden.

Wrap the caramel-coated nuts in a tea towel and
pound with a rolling pin to crush to the desired
consistency.

CHOCOLATE FUDGE PRALINE FROSTING

IF YOU'RE AFTER SOMETHING RICH, SOMETHING
A LITTLE DECADENT, TRY THIS SMALL TASTE
OF CARAMELIZED HEAVEN. THIS FROSTING
WILL ENRICH YOUR FAVORITE CAKE, BE IT
VANILLA, CHOCOLATE, HAZELNUT, OR COFFEE.

To fill and frost an 8-inch (20-cm) round cake
Preparation time: 10 minutes

$1/2$ lb (250 g) best-quality dark and milk chocolate
  (or $1/4$ lb/125 g each), broken into pieces
$1/2$ cup less 1 Tbsp (100 mL) finely ground praline powder
$1/4$ cup (50 mL) unsalted butter
2 Tbsp (30 mL) water

Combine all the ingredients either in a microwaveable bowl and soften in the microwave or in a
heatproof bowl over a saucepan of barely simmering
water. Stir until glossy and then let the frosting set
slightly before using so that it holds its shape and
doesn't trickle off the sides of the cake.

If you prefer, cut the cake in half horizontally and
spread the cut side of one half with some of the
frosting. Place the other half on top, cut side down,
and frost the sides and top of the cake, using a
rubber spatula or a long thin metal spatula. Let
yourself go—make wild patterns in the frosting,
or just smooth it over if that's what you fancy.

SALTED BUTTER CARAMEL ICE CREAM

IT WAS A REVOLUTION WHEN ONE OF THE
MAIN COMMERCIAL ICE-CREAM BRANDS IN
FRANCE BROUGHT OUT A SALTED BUTTER
CARAMEL ICE CREAM. AT MY HOUSE THIS
COMPLETELY TRANSFORMED APPLE PIES AND
COMPOTES, AND SERVED AS INSPIRATION
FOR CREATING DOZENS OF SAUCES TO POUR
OVER IT: BUTTERSCOTCH, CHOCOLATE FUDGE,
AND SO ON. BUT MOST OF THE TIME, I SERVE
IT ON ITS OWN, WITH MAYBE JUST A FEW
COOKIES. IT USED TO BE THAT ONLY THE
TOP-END-OF-THE-MARKET ICE-CREAM BRANDS
HAD SUCH FASHIONABLE FLAVORS, BUT
COMMERCIAL SALTED BUTTER CARAMEL ICE
CREAM IS NOW READILY AVAILABLE AND MAKES
IT EASY TO DRESS UP AND PERSONALIZE ANY
NUMBER OF DESSERTS. THE ONLY THING LEFT
TO DO, GIVEN THE CHOICE OF FLAVORS ON
OFFER IN THE STORES, IS TO TRY MAKING
THEM AT HOME. THIS VERSION MUST BE
SERVED STRAIGHT FROM THE ICE-CREAM
MAKER, FRESHLY MADE, WHICH IS WHAT
MAKES HOMEMADE ICE CREAM SUPERIOR TO
STORE-BOUGHT.

Serves 6
Preparation time: 10 minutes
Cooking time: 15 minutes
Ice-cream churning time: 30 minutes approx

5 egg yolks
2 Tbsp (30 mL) superfine sugar, for the ice cream
2 cups (500 mL) whipping cream
**1/2 cup less 1 Tbsp (100 mL) granulated sugar,
   for the caramel**
2 Tbsp (30 mL) water
1/4 cup (50 mL) salted butter

In a heatproof bowl, beat the egg yolks with the
2 Tbsp of superfine sugar until thick and pale
yellow in color, and doubled in volume.

In a heavy-bottomed saucepan, bring 1 1/4 cups
(300 mL) of the cream to a boil and pour over
the egg and sugar mixture, whisking constantly.
Return this to the saucepan and cook over low
heat, stirring constantly with a wooden spoon,
until it's thick and coats the back of the spoon.
Remove from the heat and let cool.

In another heavy-bottomed saucepan, make a
caramel with the 1/2 cup less 1 Tbsp granulated
sugar and the 2 Tbsp (30 mL) water (see page 12).
Remove from the heat and add the butter and the
remaining cream. Return to the heat to melt any
sugar crystals that may have formed.

Combine the custard and caramel mixtures.
Let cool completely before transferring to the
bowl of an ice-cream maker and churn to maker's
instructions. Serve as soon as it's ready.

ALMOST CHEATING VERSION

Make a basic Vanilla Ice Cream (see page 40) then
add store-bought caramel sauce, or homemade if
you have some, and a pat of salted butter before
churning in the ice-cream maker.

DEFINITELY CHEATING VERSION

Use best-quality store-bought vanilla ice cream,
let it soften a little, and then swirl in store-bought
caramel sauce.

CARAMEL CANDY ICE CREAM

Serves 6

**1 quantity of Vanilla Ice Cream (see page 40) or
   best quality store-bought**
1–2 soft caramel candy bars, cut into small pieces
1 1/4 cups (300 mL) Caramel Candy Sauce (see page 44)

Make the Vanilla Ice Cream according to the recipe
on page 40, or allow the container of store-bought
ice cream to soften slightly. Add pieces of soft
caramel candy bars to the ice cream.

Serve scoops of the ice cream with the Caramel
Candy Sauce poured over.

CARAMEL + PLEASURE

CARAMEL IS APPEALING, WITHOUT A DOUBT. HOWEVER, IT CAN SOMETIMES BE OVERLY SWEET. THIS SELECTION OF RECIPES SERVES AS A BLANK CANVAS FOR CARAMEL, TO HELP TONE DOWN THE SWEETNESS (NOT NECESSARILY THE CALORIES, BUT THAT'S NOT THE POINT!), AND INCREASE THE PLEASURE.

VANILLA ICE CREAM

This is a perfect excuse for making caramel sauce, on its own or with a crushed-up caramel candy bar added as well. It's worth investing in a small ice-cream maker. All that's left is to time it carefully and then serve straight from the machine.

Serves 6
Preparation time: 20 minutes
Chilling time: 2 hours
Ice-cream churning time: 20 minutes approx

5 egg yolks
1/3 cup (75 mL) granulated sugar
**2 cups (500 mL) whipping cream, or a mixture
  of whipping cream and whole milk**
**1 vanilla bean, split in half lengthwise,
  seeds scraped out and set aside**

In a heatproof bowl, beat the egg yolks and sugar until light and pale yellow in color, and doubled in volume.

In a large heavy-bottomed saucepan, combine the cream, or cream and milk (if using), the vanilla bean and its seeds, and bring just to a boil.

Pour the hot cream onto the egg yolks whisking vigorously. Return the mixture to the saucepan and cook over low heat, stirring constantly with a wooden spoon, for about 3 minutes until it is thick and coats the back of the spoon.

Remove the pan from the heat and set aside to cool, then chill in the refrigerator before transferring to the ice-cream machine to churn for about 20 minutes or until ready.

I always leave the vanilla bean in until the last minute to extract the maximum flavor, but don't forget to remove it before churning.

CRÈME FRAÎCHE SORBET

THIS IS SIMPLY BEST QUALITY CRÈME FRAÎCHE THAT HAS BEEN INCORPORATED INTO CUSTARD SAUCE FOR A BIT OF SWEETNESS. THE IDEA IS TO GET FRESHNESS AND A PLEASANT TOUCH OF ACIDITY TO BALANCE OUT THE SWEETNESS OF CARAMEL. IF YOU DON'T HAVE ENOUGH TIME TO MAKE A SORBET, THEN CRÈME FRAÎCHE, MASCARPONE, OR THICK, CREAMY PLAIN YOGURT STRAIGHT FROM THE REFRIGERATOR AND ON THEIR OWN ARE JUST AS GOOD.

Serves 6
Ice-cream churning time: 20 minutes approx

1 cup (250 mL) crème fraîche, whole fat not fat-free
**2 Tbsp (30 mL) stirring custard (crème anglaise)
  or 2 egg yolks and 1 Tbsp superfine sugar**

Put all the ingredients in an ice-cream maker and churn for about 20 minutes or until set. Serve immediately.

VARIATION

MASCARPONE OR YOGURT SORBET

Use 1 cup (250 mL) mascarpone or thick, creamy plain yogurt in place of the crème fraîche.

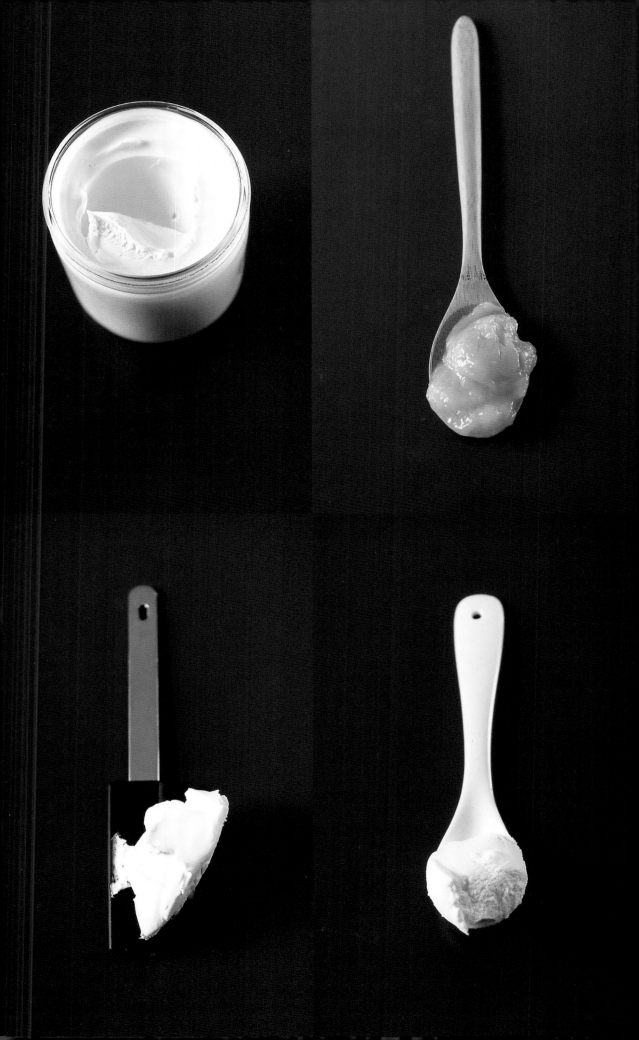

A SELECTION OF CARAMEL CANDIES
(AN INCOMPLETE LIST)

YOU WILL ALL HAVE YOUR OWN FAVORITE CARAMEL CANDIES AND BARS, BUT HERE ARE SOME OF MINE. THEY ARE BOTH DELICIOUS AND USEFUL!

CURLY WURLY

These chewy chocolate-coated caramel bars (illustrated opposite, on the left) can be found in speciality stores.

In the kitchen, if you can stop yourself from eating them, you can twist the whole bar or cut bits off to use as unusual cake decorations, or melt a bar and stir into sauces.

MALTESERS

Light airy delicious little candies that have enjoyed a renaissance of late, ever since the well-known British TV chef, Jamie Oliver, crushed them up and sprinkled them over some vanilla ice cream. The idea caught on like wildfire. They have a pleasant coarse texture that grates gently on the tongue with a smooth milk chocolate coating and inimitable malted flavor.

SKOR

Skor bar is known for its delicious combination of butter toffee and milk chocolate.

Just the job, in the kitchen, for breaking into pieces to stir into ice cream, or for melting and adapting into a chocolate caramel sauce.

WERTHERS ORIGINALS

Irresistible. These hard caramels are renowned for their delicious creamy texture, and it's impossible to get enough of them. They are great when you want to really sink your teeth into something. Track them down in a specialty store.

In fact, you can have a great deal of fun sourcing butterscotch, soft caramel, and hard toffee bars, either in all their naked glory or coated with dark or milk chocolate.

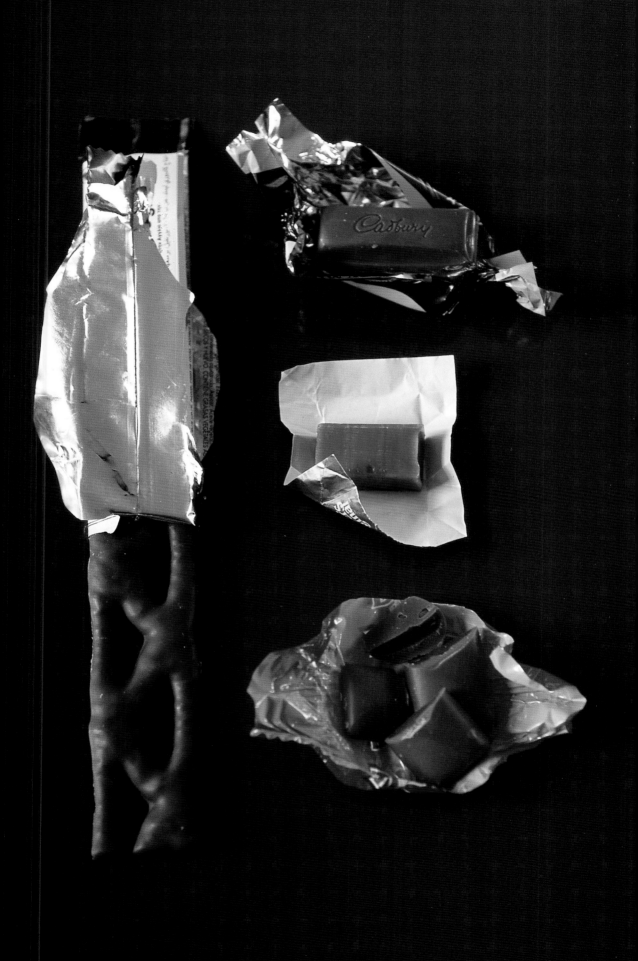

CHEAT'S SAUCES

THE WORD "CHEAT" MAY SEEM A BIT STRONG HERE. PERHAPS IT WOULD BE MORE ACCURATE TO CALL THESE "CLEVER" SAUCES—OR "ADVENTUROUS" SAUCES.

THE MAIN THING ABOUT THESE SAUCES IS THAT THERE'S NO SUGAR SYRUP TO WORRY ABOUT. ALL YOU HAVE TO DO IS TO COMBINE A FEW INGREDIENTS, HEAT THEM UP, AND YOU'LL HAVE VELVETY, DELICIOUS SAUCES.

CARAMEL CANDY SAUCE

Serves 4
Cooking time: 10 minutes

8 caramel candy pieces
1/2 cup (125 mL) whipping cream

Melt the candy pieces slowly in a non-stick pan, then stir in 1 Tbsp of cream per candy to obtain a sauce that's suitably thick when hot, or creamy when cold.

SNICKERS BAR SAUCE

Serves 4

2 Snickers bars
6 Tbsp whipping cream

Melt the Snickers bars gently in a non-stick pan, then stir in the cream and mix well. These proportions result in a very thick sauce when cooled. Add more cream if you prefer. You can also use Mars bars, just for a change!

TOFFEE SAUCE

THIS SAUCE PERFECT FOR LAST-MINUTE DESSERTS. IF YOU ALWAYS HAVE SOME GOOD-QUALITY VANILLA ICE CREAM OR SALTED BUTTER CARAMEL ICE CREAM IN YOUR FREEZER, AS WELL AS A VARIETY OF BROWN AND DEMERARA SUGARS, YOU'LL BE ABLE TO TRY A NUMBER OF DIFFERENT VARIATIONS.

ONCE THE SAUCE IS THICK, REMOVE FROM THE HEAT AND ADD A VARIETY OF INGREDIENTS: SOME DARK CHOCOLATE WITH GRATED ORANGE PEEL AND GRAND MARNIER, PRALINE PASTE AND STRONG COFFEE, PEANUT BUTTER, MAPLE SYRUP, OR VANILLA EXTRACT. THE CHOICE IS UP TO YOU.

Serves 6
Cooking time: 10 minutes

1/2 cup (125 mL) butter
2/3 cup (125 mL) demerara or soft brown sugar
2/3 cup (150 mL) whipping cream

Put all the ingredients in a saucepan and melt over low heat, stirring constantly. Simmer for a few minutes, or until the sauce is thick and darkens slightly.

A layer of butter will form on top when the sauce is chilled. Don't remove it! Simply reheat gently.

FOUR ALTERNATIVES

HONEY

This is a very useful cooking ingredient, especially when you want to caramelize cooked vegetables without having to make a sugar syrup. The only disadvantage to using honey is the absence of a burnt sugar flavor.

TREACLE

A magnificent English product that is thick, gooey, and black with a well-developed taste of licorice. Really! It's also delicious stirred into yogurt or with vanilla ice cream. It's very good in pastries or solid English puddings, but if you can't track it down in specialty stores, dark molasses poured over vanilla ice cream is pretty darn good as well.

DARK BROWN SUGARS

Demerara and the soft light and dark brown sugars always have an interesting, caramelized flavor that varies in strength depending upon the color. Paired with butter and cream and then reduced, they produce the perfect Toffee Sauce (see page 44). The easiest way to use them is sprinkled over thick, creamy yogurt and let the crystals melt into a layer of caramel.

SWEETENED CONDENSED MILK

This isn't really cheating because the sugar that goes into concentrated milk has been caramelized. It's just a matter of making life simple by taking advantage of its creamy consistency. This is a requisite for Banoffee Pie (see page 110), as well as many other recipes in this book. Watch out for spattering.

It's unwise to heat the condensed milk in its can in a pan of water. If you become absorbed in something else, the pan may run dry and the can could explode. It's safer and quicker to do the job in a microwave.

Pour 1 can (14 oz) of sweetened condensed milk into a large microwaveable bowl. Cook on MEDIUM (50% power) for 4 minutes, stirring halfway through the heating time. Reduce the power to MEDIUM–LOW (30%) and cook for 8 to 12 minutes, stirring with a wire whisk every few minutes, until thick and a light caramel color. (Microwave ovens may vary, so adjust the timing accordingly.)

If you don't have a microwave, you can pour the milk into the top of a double boiler, cover, and place over boiling water. Cook over low heat, stirring occasionally, for 40 to 50 minutes or until the milk has thickened and become a light caramel color. Beat until smooth.

TOFFEE AND MARSHMALLOW SQUARES

Makes about 20
Cooking time: 5 minutes
Refrigeration time: 1 hour

¹/₂ cup (125 mL) butter
¹/₄ lb (125 g) marshmallows
¹/₄ lb (125 g) caramel candies
7 cups (1.75 L) Rice Krispies

In a heavy-bottomed saucepan, combine the butter, marshmallows, and candies and melt over low heat.

Put the Rice Krispies in a large bowl. When the caramel mixture is smooth and well blended, pour over the cereal and mix well.

Grease a shallow 10-inch (25-cm) square pan, or use a silicone or non-stick mould. Transfer the caramel mixture to the prepared pan. Let cool completely, then cut into squares.

CARAMEL COOKIE SANDWICHES

Serves 4
Preparation time: 5 minutes
Refrigeration time: 10 minutes

5 oz (150 g) chocolate-coated caramel bars,
  broken into pieces
1 Tbsp (15 mL) whipping cream
8 butter cookies, such as shortbread

Place the chocolate-coated caramel bar pieces and cream in a heatproof bowl sitting over a saucepan of barely simmering water, or in a microwave. Stir well until smooth, then let cool. Spread some of the mixture over 4 of the cookies and top with the remaining cookies, to make a sandwich.

DOUGHNUTS FILLED WITH CARAMEL APPLESAUCE

THIS IS AN IDEAL ACTIVITY FOR COOKING WITH CHILDREN. ADULTS WILL NEED TO MAKE THE CARAMEL, BUT CHILDREN OVER THE AGE OF ABOUT 7 SHOULD BE ABLE TO HELP WITH THE APPLESAUCE.

Serves 6
Preparation time: 5 minutes
Cooking time: 10 minutes
Chilling time: 30–40 minutes

4 cooking apples, peeled, cored, and chopped
12 ready-made or store-bought small doughnuts
1 recipe quantity of Salted Butter Caramel Sauce
  (see page 30)
1 plastic syringe, or pastry bag with tip (if you have
  two of either, or even one of each, life will be easier)

Put the apples in a pan with some water and cook until soft. Transfer to a blender and reduce to a purée. Let cool completely.

Using a sharp knife, bore a hole in the doughnuts. Using the syringe or pastry bag, inject the doughnuts with some of the caramel sauce, followed by some of the applesauce. (You can now see where separate syringes, or pastry bags, for the caramel and applesauce come in handy!)

Serve immediately.

SOME LOVELY THINGS TO CRUSH UP AND SERVE WITH CARAMEL ICE CREAM

CARAMEL IS A POPULAR FLAVOR IN THE ICE-CREAM WORLD AND THE ADVENT OF CARAMEL-COATED MACADAMIA NUTS HAS MADE IT EVEN MORE INTERESTING.

CARAMEL ICE CREAM IS A RELIABLE STANDBY IN YOUR FREEZER. IT'S THE IDEAL PARTNER FOR APPLE AND PEAR HOMEMADE DESSERTS, SUCH AS TARTS AND PIES. IT'S ALSO DELICIOUS SERVED WITH CARAMELIZED APPLES OR BANANAS, NOT TO MENTION THE EFFECT IT HAS WHEN SERVED WITH A HOMEMADE TOFFEE SAUCE (SEE PAGE 44).

FOR A CARAMEL TRIPLE WHAMMY, ADD CRUNCHY CARAMEL CANDIES TO YOUR CARAMEL DESSERTS. IT'S NOW EASIER THAN EVER TO FIND A WIDE VARIETY, SO USE YOUR IMAGINATION. AND DON'T FORGET THAT YOU CAN MIX AND COMBINE SAUCES AS WELL.

TURRÓN

This is a delicious nougat from Spain, full of flavor and made with whole almonds and sesame seeds. Some varieties will need a hammer to smash them into pieces!

PEANUT BRITTLE

This is the American version of Spanish nougat and French praline. Baking soda is added to the caramel before it hardens. As a rule, I omit pharmaceutical ingredients from my recipes, with the exception of Sticky Toffee Pudding (see page 104) where it's needed with the date purée. In traditional Anglo-Saxon cuisine, baking soda is often used in cooking, especially in conjunction with butter.

MALTESERS

These are terrific on caramel ice cream because they break into millions of tiny chocolatey pieces.

MILLIONAIRE'S SHORTBREAD

THIS CONFECTION CONSISTS OF SQUARES OF SHORTBREAD COVERED IN A LAYER OF CARAMEL AND THEN A THICK TOP LAYER OF CHOCOLATE. AND ITS NAME IS AN INDICATION OF ITS RICHNESS. THESE ARE DIVINE SMASHED UP AND SPRINKLED OVER CARAMEL OR VANILLA ICE CREAM, OR ON THEIR OWN WITH A CUP OF TEA OR COFFEE.

Preparation time: 10 minutes plus 3 hours for the caramel
Cooking time: 25 minutes
Chilling time: 30–40 minutes

1 x 14-oz can sweetened condensed milk
2 cups (500 mL) all-purpose flour
$\frac{1}{3}$ cup (75 mL) granulated sugar
$\frac{1}{2}$ cup (125 mL) salted butter
6 oz (175 g) bittersweet chocolate, broken into pieces
$\frac{1}{4}$ cup (50 mL) unsalted butter

To make the caramel from condensed milk, follow one of the methods of cooking the condensed milk given on page 46. Let cool completely. Alternatively, prepare the Salted Butter Caramel Sauce on page 30.

Preheat the oven to 350°F (180°C). Grease an 8–10 inch (2–3 L) rectangular baking pan.

In the bowl of a mixer, combine the flour, sugar, and salted butter and process until the mixture resembles coarse breadcrumbs, or place in a mixing bowl and use your fingertips to combine as if making pastry.

Form into a dough, then press into the prepared pan. Bake until just golden on top.

Remove from the oven and let cool before spreading on a layer of caramel.

Melt the chocolate and unsalted butter together in a heatproof bowl set over a pan of barely simmering water, or in a microwave, and stir well until smooth. Pour over the caramel layer and smooth with a palette knife.

To serve, let harden completely, then cut into squares.

MARTINE'S FAMOUS HONEY CHOCOLATE CARAMELS

IN THE TINY FRENCH VILLAGE OF MISSILLAC, IN BRITTANY, NEWS TRAVELS
FAST WHEN MARTINE STARTS TO MAKE A BATCH OF CARAMELS. THE CLEVEREST
GO STRAIGHT TO HER HOME IN THE HOPE OF SCRAPING THE SIDES OF THE
PAN WHILE THE CARAMEL IS STILL SOFT AND WARM. EVERYONE ELSE WAITS
AND HAS THEM AS AN AFTER-SCHOOL SNACK, OR AFTER A DINNER PARTY. BUT
MOSTLY EVERYONE WAITS FOR THE NEXT BATCH. THERE'S NEVER ENOUGH TO
GO AROUND.

Makes about 40 caramels
Cooking time: 20 minutes

½ cup less 1 Tbsp (100 mL) granulated sugar
½ lb (250 g) best-quality bittersweet chocolate, broken into pieces
1 cup (250 mL) 2% milk
1 Tbsp (15 mL) salted butter
1 Tbsp (15 mL) honey

Have ready a non-stick shallow pan, or one lined with a silicone liner or parchment
paper, approximately 7–8-inch (18–20 cm) square.

Put the sugar in a pan, sprinkle over a few drops of water, and heat gently until it
forms a syrup. Bring to a boil and add the chocolate. Stir well so it melts without
burning. Add the milk and stir well. Bring to a boil, then lower the heat and simmer
gently, stirring constantly with a wooden spoon.

Add the butter and honey and simmer for 10–15 minutes more—keep stirring and
scraping the sides so the caramel doesn't stick.

The caramel will thicken quickly at the end of the cooking time. Beat well at this stage
and test the consistency by letting it drop from the spoon (it takes time to develop an
eye as good as Martine's for this!). As soon as the caramel stops falling off the spoon,
or it begins to slow down, pour it into the pan and level it out. As it begins to harden,
cut into squares. Allow 1 hour before the caramels are ready.

These may be too hard or too soft the first time you make them, but they will always
be delicious and made by you (and thanks to Martine for the recipe!).

FUDGE

FUDGE, WHICH IS ALSO CALLED "TABLET" IN SCOTLAND, IS A SORT OF CRYSTALLIZED BUTTER CARAMEL THAT CRUNCHES BEAUTIFULLY BEFORE MELTING ON THE TONGUE. BE WARNED THAT THIS REQUIRES 10 MINUTES OF VIGOROUS BEATING, BUT IT'S WELL WORTH THE EFFORT.

Makes about 20 pieces
Preparation time: 15 minutes
Cooking time: 30 minutes

2 cups (500 mL) granulated sugar
1/4 cup plus 1 Tbsp (65 mL) salted butter
1/4 cup (50 mL) sweetened condensed milk
3/4 cup (175 mL) water

Have ready a non-stick shallow pan, or one lined with a silicone liner or parchment paper, approximately 9-inch (23-cm) square.

Put all the ingredients in a large heavy-bottomed saucepan over low heat until the butter and sugar are completely dissolved.

Bring just to a boil, stirring constantly so the fudge doesn't stick to the bottom of the pan. Simmer gently for about 10 minutes, until the soft-ball stage is reached (this is when a little piece of the mixture forms into a soft ball when dropped into cold water). The color should have turned from white to golden caramel.

Remove the pan from the heat and let cool for about 5 minutes, then beat vigorously with a wooden spoon for 5–10 minutes until it begins to harden.

Transfer to the prepared pan, where it will continue to harden, but before it completely sets, cut into bite-sized pieces and let cool.

VARIATIONS

WITH DRIED CRANBERRIES

Add 1/3 cup (30 g) dried cranberries to the fudge mixture after beating.

WITH CHOCOLATE

Add 2 tsp (10 mL) cocoa powder to the mixture at the beginning of cooking.

WITH BRAZIL NUTS

Add 4–5 chopped Brazil nuts to the fudge mixture after beating.

SWEET TREATS

THREE SIMPLE WAYS TO SERVE CARAMELIZED BANANAS

IT'S A MATCH MADE IN HEAVEN. CARAMEL AND BANANAS GO SO WELL TOGETHER. BANANAS CARAMELIZE QUICKLY ONCE THEY COME INTO CONTACT WITH SOME BUTTER AND SUGAR IN A SKILLET.

CARAMELIZED MINI-BANANA SPLITS

Serves 4
Preparation time: 3 minutes

2 oz (50 g) bittersweet chocolate, broken in pieces
4 scoops vanilla ice cream
4 mini bananas
1¹/₂ Tbsp (20 mL) butter
1 Tbsp (15 mL) granulated sugar
¹/₄ cup (50 mL) crushed pecans

Have ready 4 plates.

Melt the chocolate in a bowl set over a saucepan of barely simmering water (do not let the bowl touch the water) or in a microwave. Set aside.

Remove the ice cream from the freezer.

Slice the bananas in half lengthwise. Heat the butter and sugar in a skillet, and brown the bananas. Do not overcook or the bananas go soggy and lose their shape.

Put 1 scoop of ice cream on each of the plates. Add the bananas, the melted chocolate, and sprinkle with the pecans.

MILK CHOCOLATE TRIFLE WITH CARAMELIZED BANANAS

Serves 4
Preparation time: 15 minutes
Chilling time: 10 minutes
Refrigeration time: 2 hours

1¹/₂ Tbsp (20 mL) butter
1 Tbsp (15 mL) granulated sugar
2 bananas, sliced into rounds
1¹/₄ cups (300 mL) whipping cream
2 oz (50 g) milk chocolate, broken into pieces
4–6 ladyfingers
Dark rum or Bailey's

In a saucepan, heat the butter and sugar, then add the banana slices and cook until the bananas are caramelized. Set aside to cool.

Put half of the cream in a pan and bring just to a boil. Add the chocolate pieces and stir until smooth. Set aside.

Pour the remaining cream in a bowl and whip until firm.

Break up the ladyfingers and divide the pieces between four serving dishes. Drizzle over the rum or Bailey's and top with a layer of bananas, then a layer of chocolate cream. Chill for 10 minutes before topping with the whipped cream.

Refrigerate about 2 hours before serving.

CARAMELIZED BANANA CRÊPES FLAMBÉES

Serves 4
Preparation time: 10 minutes
Cooking time: 5 minutes, plus about 1¹/₂ hours for the crêpes

2 Tbsp (30 mL) butter
2 Tbsp (30 mL) granulated sugar
2 medium bananas, sliced into rounds
Dark rum
4 crêpes (see recipe on page 100)
Vanilla ice cream, for serving

Have ready 4 plates.

Heat the butter and sugar in a skillet and add the sliced bananas. As soon as the bananas begin to caramelize, add the rum, raise the heat and flambé by igniting.

Place a crêpe on each plate and divide the bananas between them. Drizzle over the delicious banana cooking juices, then roll or fold up.

Serve with vanilla ice cream.

THREE SIMPLE WAYS TO SERVE CARAMELIZED PINEAPPLES

AUNT BEATTIE'S EVERLASTING CAKE

THIS CAKE NEVER GOES OUT OF FASHION SINCE FASHION HASN'T QUITE REACHED ITS PLACE OF ORIGIN IN HOLLYWOOD, COUNTY DOWN, NORTHERN IRELAND. THIS RECIPE IS INSPIRED BY A SPECIALTY OF MY DEAR AUNT BEATTIE, WHO'S SO FUSSY WHEN IT COMES TO COOKING THAT SHE ACTUALLY BROUGHT HER OWN BUTTER AND IRISH SAUSAGES TO FRANCE FOR MY WEDDING.

Serves 8
Preparation time: 25 minutes
Cooking time: 25 minutes

1 large packet graham crackers, crushed
$^1/_3$ cup (75 mL) salted butter, melted
$^1/_2$ lb (250 g) pineapple, cut in pieces and caramelized in
2 Tbsp butter and 1–2 Tbsp sugar, then set aside to cool
1$^1/_4$ cups (300 mL) whipping cream
3 Tbsp (45 mL) superfine sugar
1 small milk chocolate bar, grated

In a mixing bowl, combine the graham cracker crumbs and melted butter. Transfer to a baking pan approximately 8-inch (2-L) square and press firmly to form a base.

Arrange the caramelized pineapple pieces on top. Combine the cream and sugar in a bowl and whip until firm, but not solid. Spread the whipped cream over the pineapple layer.

Decorate with the grated chocolate.

CARAMELIZED PINEAPPLE, MANGO, BANANA, AND STRAWBERRY KABOBS WITH MALIBU LIQUEUR

Serves 4
Preparation time: 15 minutes
Cooking time: 5 minutes for the caramel

$^1/_2$ cup less 1 Tbsp (100 mL) granulated sugar
2 Tbsp (30 mL) water
$^1/_4$ cup (50 mL) Malibu liqueur
2 bananas, sliced into rounds and tossed in 2–3 Tbsp
** of lemon juice**
1 mango, not too ripe, peeled and cut into cubes
$^1/_2$ pineapple, peeled and cut into cubes
12 strawberries, hulled, washed, and dried
4 metal or wooden skewers
Vanilla or coconut ice cream, to serve

Make a caramel with the sugar and water (see page 12). Remove from the heat and stir in the Malibu. Stir well, returning to the heat if necessary to dissolve any crystals that may form. Let cool while you assemble the kabobs.

Skewer the fruit, alternating the varieties, then arrange the kabobs on a serving plate. Drizzle over the caramel and serve with the ice cream.

Alternatively, make a fruit salad with the fruit pieces and drizzle with the caramel for extra crunch; omit the Malibu for a non-alcoholic option, if preferred.

CARAMELIZED PINEAPPLE WITH CARAMELIZED PINEAPPLE SAUCE

Serves 4
Preparaton time: 10 minutes

$^1/_4$ cup (50 mL) butter
1 lb (500 g) pineapple, peeled and cut in pieces (if using
** frozen pineapple, be sure to drain well and pat dry**
** with kitchen towels or the excess water will hinder**
** caramelization)**
3 Tbsp (45 mL) granulated sugar
4 slices pound cake or brioche, toasted
4 scoops vanilla ice cream

Have ready 4 dessert plates.

Heat the butter in a skillet, add the pineapple pieces, and sprinkle with the sugar to caramelize. Spoon over the pan juices while cooking.

Set aside half of the pineapple pieces. Put the remaining pineapple pieces in a blender and process until smooth and sauce-like in consistency.

Arrange the toasted cake slices on the 4 dessert plates. Place a scoop of vanilla ice cream on each slice and top with the reserved pineapple pieces. Drizzle some of the sauce over each and serve.

POACHED APPLES WITH APPLE LIQUEUR SOFT CARAMEL

APPLE LIQUEUR IS A GOOD PARTNER FOR CARAMEL, AND MANZANA VERDE LIQUEUR FROM SPAIN IS PARTICULARLY GOOD. IF YOUR LIQUOR STORE DOESN'T STOCK IT, THEY SHOULD BE ABLE TO SUGGEST A GOOD ALTERNATIVE BRAND.

Serves 4
Cooking time: 10 minutes
Refrigeration time: about 1 hour

4 small apples (Golden Delicious, McIntosh …)
1 Tbsp (15 mL) lemon juice
$1/2$ cup less 1 Tbsp (100 mL) granulated sugar
2 Tbsp (30 mL) water
$1/3$ cup (75 mL) Manzana or other apple liqueur
Italian biscotti, or butter cookies, for serving

Carefully peel the apples, retaining the stem in place and leaving them whole.

Bring a saucepan of water to a boil, add the lemon juice and the apples, and poach for 4–5 minutes. The apples should soften (test with a skewer) but still retain their shape. Remove from the water with a slotted spoon, drain on kitchen towels, and let cool.

In a heavy-bottomed saucepan, combine the sugar and water and make a deep golden caramel (see page 12). Remove from the heat and stir in the Manzana, then return to the heat, stirring to dissolve any crystals that may form. Let cool.

Just before serving, pour the caramel over the poached apples and serve with Italian biscotti or butter cookies.

NORMANDY TRIFLE

Serves 4
Preparation time: 10 minutes
Cooking time: 10 minutes
Refrigeration time: 3–4 hours

4 apples (Golden Delicious, McIntosh …) peeled, cored, and cut in quarters
2 Tbsp (30 mL) granulated sugar
1 cup (250 mL) whipping cream
2 Tbsp (30 mL) mascarpone
6–8 all-butter cookies, or shortbread, crumbled
$1/4$ cup (50 mL) Calvados
$1/3$ cup (75 mL) Salted Butter Caramel Sauce (see page 30)

Put the apples in a saucepan with the sugar and cook, covered, adding a splash of water as necessary, until completely soft. Transfer to a blender and purée, or push through a sieve.

Combine the whipping cream and mascarpone in a bowl and whip until firm but not solid.

In 4 serving glasses, arrange a layer of crumbled cookies and drizzle with Calvados. Add a layer of apple purée, caramel sauce, and mascarpone cream. Add further layers to use up the ingredients, as illustrated opposite, finishing with a layer of caramel sauce and a dollop of mascarpone cream.

Refrigerate for at least 3–4 hours before serving.

Alternatively, increase the quantities and serve the trifle in a large glass bowl.

WHAT TO DO WITH A JAR OF DULCE DE LECHE

IF THIS IS A NEW INGREDIENT TO YOU, IT'S A THICK CARAMEL TOFFEE SAUCE USUALLY SOLD IN JARS IN FINE FOOD STORES OR THE SPECIALTY SECTION OF GOOD SUPERMARKETS.

YOU COULD START BY MAKING THE BANOFFEE PIE ON PAGE 116, OR YOU COULD MIX DULCE DE LECHE WITH SOME PLAIN YOGURT AND ADD IT TO YOUR VANILLA ICE CREAM. YOU COULD EVEN SIMPLY SPREAD IT ON A HALVED BAGUETTE, SANDWICH STYLE.

DENISE, A CHILEAN FRIEND OF MINE, TELLS ME THAT IN HER COUNTRY THIS IS CALLED "MANJAR" AND IT'S ONE OF HER FAVORITE INGREDIENTS. SHE MAKES IT SOUND AS IF IT'S THE PRIDE AND JOY OF HER DELIGHTFUL COUNTRY! AT THE SCHOOL HER BOYS ATTEND, THEIR BIRTHDAYS ARE ALWAYS ANTICIPATED WITH EXCITEMENT AS EVERY YEAR DENISE SENDS THEM IN WITH HER FAMOUS DULCE DE LECHE AND RASPBERRY JAM CAKE TO MARK THE OCCASION. THIS IS A VERSION OF THAT RECIPE, SINCE THE REAL THING IS A WELL-GUARDED SECRET, OF COURSE.

DENISE'S CAKE, ALMOST

Serves 10–12
Preparation time: 15 minutes
Cooking time: up to 40 minutes

4 sheets store-bought puff pastry, each rolled out if necessary and trimmed to a 10-inch (25 cm) diameter disk
2 Tbsp (30 mL) melted butter
2 jars dulce de leche, or 3 cans sweetened condensed milk, cooked by one of the methods on page 46
1 jar best-quality raspberry conserve

Preheat the oven to 350°F (180°C).

Brush the pastry sheets with the melted butter and bake on cookie sheets for 20 minutes, or until golden. Bake all at once if your oven allows, otherwise work in batches.

Remove from the oven and let cool completely on racks.

Place a cooled pastry disk on a large serving plate and spread over a layer of dulce de leche, top with another pastry disk and spread it with a layer of raspberry conserve. Top with the third pastry disk and spread it with dulce de leche.

Crumble the remaining pastry disk (leaving some to sprinkle on the top at the end) and mix with 2–3 Tbsp (45 mL) of dulce de leche and spread over the top to make it look "nice and smooth," says Denise. Sprinkle over the remaining pastry crumbs.

DULCE DE LECHE WITH MERINGUE APPLES

ANOTHER QUICK AND EASY RECIPE FROM CHILE.

Serves 8
Preparation time: 20 minutes
Cooking time: 10 minutes

8 apples (Golden Delicious, McIntosh ...) peeled, cored, and cut in quarters
Ground cinnamon
5 egg whites
1/4 cup (50 mL) superfine sugar
1 jar dulce de leche (or 2 cans sweetened condensed milk cooked by one of the methods on page 46)

Preheat the oven to 350°F (180°C).

Put the pieces of apple in a saucepan with some water and a pinch of cinnamon and cook, covered, adding a splash of water as necessary, for about 10 minutes or until completely soft.

Put the egg whites in a bowl with half of the sugar. Beat until soft peaks form, add the remaining sugar and beat until stiff and glossy.

Transfer the cooked apples to a baking dish and spread evenly. Spread over a layer of dulce de leche, then top with the meringue.

Bake until the meringue just begins to brown and serve immediately.

CARAMEL, APPLE, PRUNE, AND YOGURT SUNDAE

Serves 4
Cooking time: 25 minutes
Refrigeration time: 1 hour, if you make the applesauce, otherwise 10 minutes

4 apples (Golden Delicious, McIntosh ...), peeled, cored, and cut in quarters, or 2 small jars unsweetened applesauce (homemade is always better!)
8–10 large, juicy, pitted prunes, or ready-made prune purée
1¼ cups (300 mL) thick, creamy yogurt
¼ cup (50 mL) Salted Butter Caramel Sauce (see page 30)
Cookies or Italian biscotti

Put the apples in a saucepan with a splash of water. Cook, covered, until soft, about 10 minutes. Purée in a blender, or push through a sieve, and let cool.

Put the prunes in a saucepan with a little water. Cook, covered, for about 5 minutes or until soft. Purée in a blender until smooth, or push through a sieve.

In 4 sundae glasses, arrange alternate layers of all the ingredients and serve with almond or ginger cookies, or Italian biscotti.

CARAMEL SUNDAE

Serves 4
Preparation time: 10 minutes

¾ cup (175 mL) whipping cream
Vanilla extract
3 Tbsp (45 mL) superfine sugar
2 cups (500 mL) caramel ice cream
2 cups (500 mL) vanilla ice cream
4 slices pound cake, cut in pieces
Ready-made caramel sauce (2 Tbsp per glass)
¼ cup (50 g) crushed caramelized hazelnuts (see Praline page 36)
¼ cup (50 g) chopped hazelnuts

Combine the cream, a few drops of vanilla extract, and the sugar in a bowl and beat until firm, but not solid.

Remove the ice cream from the freezer to soften.

Arrange the cake pieces in the bottom of 4 tall sundae glasses. Drizzle each with the caramel sauce. In each glass build up the layers as follows: a scoop of vanilla ice cream, a sprinkle of caramelized hazelnuts, a drizzle of caramel sauce, a scoop of caramel ice cream, a sprinkle of caramelized hazelnuts, a drizzle of caramel sauce. Top each with a dollop of the whipped cream and a scattering of chopped hazelnuts and serve immediately.

APRICOT AND CARAMEL CREAM SUNDAE

Serves 4
Preparation time: 15 minutes
Cooking time: 15 minutes

For the apricot
1¼ lb (625 g) ready-made apricot purée, unsweetened if possible

For the caramel cream
2 Tbsp (30 mL) superfine sugar
4 egg yolks
1½ Tbsp (20 mL) all-purpose flour, sifted
⅔ cup (150 mL) whipping cream
⅔ cup (150 mL) whole milk
½ cup less 1 Tbsp (100 mL) granulated sugar
2 Tbsp (30 mL) water
Caramel-coated fruit, optional (see page 20)

In a bowl, beat together the 2 Tbsp superfine sugar, egg yolks, and flour until the mixture is light and pale yellow in color and doubled in volume. Set aside.

In a saucepan, combine the cream and milk and bring just to a boil.

Make a caramel from the remaining sugar and the water (see page 12). Remove from the heat and stir in the cream mixture. Stir well, then return to the heat and continue stirring to dissolve any crystals that may form.

Pour the caramel cream over the egg and sugar mixture, stirring vigorously. Return to the saucepan, bring to a boil and simmer for 1 minute, stirring constantly with a wooden spoon until the mixture thickens and coats the back of the spoon.

Let cool completely.

In 4 tall sundae glasses, arrange alternate layers of the apricot purée and the caramel cream. Decorate with caramel-coated fruit if desired.

MAGNIFICENT TRIFLE

THIS RECIPE COMES FROM A FAVORITE HOTEL (HOTEL COSTES), WHICH HAS
BEEN A LONG-STANDING ENTHUSIAST OF THIS TYPICALLY ENGLISH DESSERT.
IT'S ALMOST AS GOOD AS THEIR CRÊPES AND CERTAINLY GENEROUS ENOUGH TO
FEED A LARGE GROUP OF CATWALK MODELS FOR ONE WEEK.

Serves 4
Preparation time: 20 minutes
Refrigeration time: 2–3 hours

For the caramel
1/2 cup (50 g) pine nuts
1/2 cup less 1 Tbsp (100 mL) granulated sugar
2 Tbsp (30 mL) water
2 Tbsp (30 mL) granola

For the trifle
3/4 cup (175 mL) whipping cream
2 Tbsp (30 mL) mascarpone
1 Tbsp (15 mL) superfine sugar
1/2 tsp (2 mL) vanilla extract
8 slices pound cake or 1 dozen ladyfingers, broken in pieces
1/4 cup (50 mL) pear liqueur
8 pear halves in syrup, drained
Ready-made or store-bought caramel sauce

For the caramel, toast the pine nuts in a dry skillet and set aside to cool. Make a
caramel with the sugar and water (see page 12). Toss together the toasted pine nuts
and granola and spoon 4 mounds onto a silicone baking sheet liner or parchment
paper. Pour over the caramel. Spread out into nice rounds and leave to set.

In a bowl, combine the cream, mascarpone, sugar, and vanilla extract. Beat until firm,
but not solid.

Divide the cake or ladyfinger pieces between 4 tall sundae glasses. Drizzle each with
the pear liqueur, top with a pear half, and spoon in some caramel sauce. Add a layer
of whipped cream. Repeat the layers, finishing with a layer of whipped cream.

Refrigerate for at least 2–3 hours.

Before serving, place a caramelized-nut mound on top of each sundae.

MASCARPONE MOUSSE WITH
CARAMELIZED GRANOLA

Serves 6

$^3/_4$ cup (175 mL) whipping cream
$^1/_4$ cup (50 mL) mascarpone
2 egg yolks
Seeds scraped from 1 vanilla bean
$^2/_3$ cup (150 mL) icing (confectioner's) sugar
$^1/_4$ cup (125 mL) granola
$^1/_2$ cup less 1 Tbsp (100 mL) granulated sugar
2 Tbsp (30 mL) water

In a large mixing bowl, combine the cream, mascarpone, egg yolks, vanilla bean seeds, and icing sugar. Beat until firm.

Transfer to six pretty serving glasses and refrigerate until needed.

Crush the granola to a powder in an electric grinder or with a rolling pin. Spread the powdered granola on a baking sheet lined with a silicone liner or parchment paper.

Put the sugar and water in a saucepan and make a caramel (see page 12). Pour the caramel over the granola powder. Let harden, then crush to a powder with a rolling pin.

Just before serving, stir the caramelized granola into the mousse. Alternatively, it can be served separately.

If you pop the empty vanilla bean into a screw-top jar filled with sugar, after a few weeks you'll have a supply of vanilla sugar.

MILK CHOCOLATE MOUSEE WITH
SALTED BUTTER CARAMEL

Serves 6
Preparation time: 10 minutes
Cooking time: 20 minutes
Refrigeration time: 4–5 hours or overnight

$^1/_2$ cup less 1 Tbsp (100 mL) granulated sugar
2 Tbsp (30 mL) water
2 Tbsp (30 mL) salted butter
$^3/_4$ cup (175 mL) whipping cream
7 oz (200 g) best-quality Continental milk chocolate, at least 38% cocoa solids,
   broken in pieces
3 eggs, separated

Make a caramel with the granulated sugar and the water (see page 12). Remove
from the heat, stir in the butter and cream, then return to the heat and cook until
smooth.

Let cool slightly then stir in the pieces of chocolate. Mix well until smooth and let
cool completely.

Beat in the egg yolks. In another bowl, beat the egg whites until they hold stiff
peaks, then fold carefully into the chocolate mixture.

Transfer to individual serving bowls, or one large bowl, and refrigerate for at least
4–5 hours. It's even better if you make it a day in advance.

FLOATING ISLANDS

Serves 6–8
Preparation time: 30 minutes
Cooking time: 20 minutes

For the "islands" and "custard sea"
2 cups (500 mL) whole milk
1½ cups (300 mL) whipping cream
1 vanilla bean, split lengthwise, seeds scraped out
  and set aside
10 eggs, separated
¾ cup (175 mL) granulated sugar
¼ cup (50 mL) superfine sugar
2 cups (500 mL) milk, for poaching if using that method

For the caramel
½ cup less 1 Tbsp (100 mL) granulated sugar
2 Tbsp (30 mL) water

In a large heavy-bottomed saucepan, combine the milk, cream, vanilla bean, and its seeds and bring just to a boil.

Meanwhile, put the egg yolks in a large heatproof mixing bowl with the ¾ cup granulated sugar and whisk until light, pale yellow in color and doubled in volume.

Pour the hot milk mixture onto the egg yolk mixture, stirring vigorously, then return to the saucepan and cook over medium heat, stirring constantly with a wooden spoon, until the mixture is thick enough to coat the back of the spoon. Remove from the heat; the mixture will continue to cook because of the residual heat.

Let cool completely. Leave the vanilla bean in the custard during cooling to increase the flavor.

Put the egg whites in a large mixing bowl with the ¼ cup of superfine sugar. Beat into stiff peaks. Scoop out the number of mounds required for the diners with a large metal spoon and shape the top of the "islands" with another spoon. Poach the mounds in the microwave, or in simmering milk (see below).

Microwave method: Put the mounds directly on a glass plate or tray and cook on HIGH for about 10 seconds. They will puff up when cooked.

Milk poaching method: Pour 2 cups of milk into a deep skillet, heat to simmering, and poach one or two mounds at a time, turning them regularly. Transfer to drain on kitchen towels and cool.

About 1 hour before serving, make the caramel with the sugar and water (see page 12).

To serve, either pour the custard sauce into a large shallow serving dish and top with all the "islands," or pour some of the custard sauce into individual dessert plates and top with one or two "islands." Drizzle over the caramel while it's still hot and let cool before serving.

Alternatively, you can make pulled caramel strands (see page 16). This is more complicated; you must wait until the caramel has cooled enough so that you can handle it without burning your fingertips but while it's still supple enough to be pulled. It can be reheated if necessary.

This dessert needs to be served soon after the caramel strands have been put over the "islands," since the pulled caramel will not stay crispy for long, especially if it's refrigerated, as the humidity will soften the caramel.

APPLE "SOUP" WITH THE BEST SALTED BUTTER CARAMEL IN THE WORLD

THIS MAY NOT LOOK LIKE ANYTHING SPECIAL, BUT AS THE BEST SALTED BUTTER CARAMEL IN THE WORLD IS HOMEMADE, I PROMISE YOU IT'S AN ABSOLUTE DELIGHT!

Serves 6
Preparation time: 5 minutes

4 cups (1 L) best-quality apple juice
3–4 Tbsp Salted Butter Caramel Sauce (see page 30)
Thin slices of dessert apple or pear, for serving
Whipped cream flavored with Calvados (optional)

Nice things to serve with the "soup"
Toasted pound cake slices, all-butter cookies, shortbread, French Toast flavored with nutmeg...

Don't prepare the fruit until you're ready to serve, otherwise it will start to discolor.

Put the apple juice in a saucepan and heat until warm. Add the Salted Butter Caramel Sauce. Stir well to combine.

Serve hot, but not too hot, with the fruit slices, and the whipped cream (if using). This looks very attractive in pretty serving bowls and makes the ideal ending to both an all-soup meal or following a single course, but a substantial one!

CARAMELIZED LEMON TART

Serves 4
Preparation time: 30 minutes
Chilling time for the pastry: 1 hour
Cooking time: 40 minutes cooking time

For the pastry
**$^1/_2$ cup less 1 Tbsp (100 mL), unsalted butter at room
  temperature, cut into cubes**
$1^1/_4$ cups (150 mL) all-purpose flour
1 Tbsp (15 mL) icing (confectioner's) sugar
1 Tbsp (15 mL) ice water

For the lemon filling
Grated rind and juice of 5 medium lemons (or 4 large)
$^2/_3$ cup (150 mL) superfine sugar
6 eggs
$1^3/_4$ cups (425 mL) whipping cream

For the topping
Icing (confectioner's) sugar, for caramelizing

To make the pastry, combine the butter, flour, and sugar in a food processor and process until the mixture resembles coarse crumbs. Alternatively, put the ingredients in a mixing bowl and combine them with your fingertips. Add sufficient of the water to bind into a dough, form it into a ball, and refrigerate for 1 hour.

Preheat the oven to 350°F (180°C) and put a baking sheet in to heat up.

Roll out the pastry thinly to line the base and sides of a 9-inch (23-cm) flan pan with a removable bottom. Chill in the refrigerator for 30 minutes, then remove and bake blind (see TIP below) in the oven on the baking sheet for 12 minutes, then remove the pie weights or beans and continue to bake until the pastry turns a light gold color.

Remove the pastry crust shell from the oven but do not remove from the flan pan. Reduce the temperature to 300°F (150°C).

For the filling, put the lemon zest and juice and the sugar into a saucepan and heat very gently just until the sugar has dissolved. Set aside.

In a large mixing bowl, beat the eggs with the cream and then pour into a heavy-bottomed saucepan. Heat very gently over low heat, the mixture must not boil, stirring continuously with a wooden spoon until the mixture begins to thicken and coat the back of the spoon. Stir in the warm lemon syrup, mix well, and pour into the pie crust shell. (The easiest way to prevent spills while taking the filled shell to the oven is to first pour the filling into a large pitcher, place the pie crust shell in the oven, then pull out the rack a little way and pour the filling into the shell.)

Bake for about 35 minutes or until the filling is set but feels springy in the center. Leave to cool then chill completely in the refrigerator.

Just before serving, sift a layer of icing sugar over the surface of the filling and caramelize with a kitchen blow torch, or quickly under a preheated broiler.

TIP To bake blind, fit the rolled out pastry firmly into the baking pan, smoothing down to prevent trapped air. Place on top a piece of parchment paper or aluminum foil, large enough to reach up the sides of the pastry lining. Add pie weights or dried beans and bake for about 15 minutes of the total baking time. After which, remove the weights and the paper and continue to bake for the remaining specified time.

DARK CHOCOLATE AND SOFT CARAMEL TART WITH TOASTED ALMOND PASTRY

THE CONTRAST BETWEEN THE STRENGTH OF DARK CHOCOLATE AND THE TENDER SWEETNESS OF CARAMEL IS HIGHLIGHTED IN THIS VERY RICH TART. THE SLIGHTLY SWEET PASTRY WITH A CRUNCH OF ALMONDS IS THE PERFECT BACKGROUND FOR THE STARS IN THIS RECIPE.

Serves 8–10
Preparation time: 40 minutes
Refrigeration time: 3 hours
Cooking time: 25 minutes

For the pastry
1½ cups (375 mL) all-purpose flour
½ cup (50 g) slivered almonds, dry roasted and cooled
2 Tbsp (30 mL) icing (confectioner's) sugar
½ cup less 1 Tbsp (100 mL) unsalted butter, chilled and cut into small cubes

For the filling
4–5 Tbsp soft caramel (see page 30)
7 oz (200 g) bittersweet chocolate, broken into pieces
¼ cup (50 mL) unsalted butter
Whipped cream, to serve

For the pastry, put the flour, almonds, sugar, and butter in the bowl of a food processor and process until the mixture resembles coarse crumbs. Alternatively, put the ingredients in a mixing bowl and combine them with your fingertips. Add sufficient water to make a dough and form into a ball. Wrap in plastic wrap and refrigerate for 1 hour.

Roll out the pastry and line the base and sides of a 9-inch (23-cm) flan pan and chill in the refrigerator for another 30 minutes.

Preheat the oven to 350°F (180°C) and put a baking sheet in the oven to heat up.

Remove the pastry shell from the refrigerator and bake blind (see TIP on page 82) in the oven on the baking sheet for 12 minutes, then remove the pie weights or beans and continue to bake until the pie crust shell is golden. Remove from the oven and cool completely.

Spread the caramel in the cooled tart shell.

Melt the chocolate and butter together in a heatproof bowl set over a pan of barely simmering water, or in a microwave. Stir until smooth. Spread evenly over the caramel layer and refrigerate for at least 2 hours.

Serve in thin slices, accompanied by the whipped cream.

BANANA AND DRIED MANGO "TARTE TATIN"

IT'S EASIER THAN EVER TO FIND SOFT AND TENDER DRIED FRUIT. THE INTENSE FLAVOR AND TEXTURE OF MANY OF THE VARIETIES AVAILABLE GO WELL WITH COOKED BANANAS, BUT IF YOU CAN'T FIND ANY DRIED MANGOES, THEN DATES, PRUNES, OR APRICOTS ARE ALL GOOD SUBSTITUTES.

Serves 6–8
Preparation time: 5 minutes
Cooking time: 35 minutes

$^2/_3$ cup (150 mL) granulated sugar
$^1/_4$ cup (50 mL) salted butter
3–4 medium bananas
6–8 very tender pieces of dried mango
1 package puff pastry
Whipped cream or sorbet (see page 40), to serve

Caramelize the sugar with a splash of water (see page 12) in a flameproof metal tarte Tatin pan, or a suitable-sized skillet capable of being placed in a hot oven. Add the butter and let it melt in slowly, stirring gently to distribute evenly. Remove from the heat.

Cut the bananas into 1-inch (2.5 cm) thick rounds. Arrange the banana slices in the caramel and put the mango pieces in between. Roll out the pastry in a circle larger than the diameter of the pan and lay it on top of the fruit, tucking in the edges down between the fruit and the pan sides.

Bake for 30–40 minutes, or until golden.

Remove from the oven and let stand for 5 minutes. Turn the tart out of the pan by placing the serving plate face down on the pie crust lid and, while holding it firmly in place, quickly turn the pan over. If any of the fruit pieces stay attached to the pan after you've flipped it out, simply remove them from the pan and stick them back in place.

Serve accompanied by whipped cream or sorbet.

QUICK APPLE "TARTE TATIN" WITH SALTED BUTTER CARAMEL

Serves 6
Preparation time: 10 minutes
Cooking time: 30 minutes

$^1/_2$ cup less 1 Tbsp (100 mL) granulated sugar
$^1/_4$ cup (50 mL) salted butter
4–5 apples (Golden Delicious, McIntosh ...), peeled, cored, and cut in quarters
1 package puff pastry, rolled in to a circle

Preheat the oven to 350°F (180°C).

Caramelize the sugar with a splash of water (see page 12) in a flameproof metal tatin pan, or a suitable-sized skillet capable of being placed in a hot oven. Remove from the heat and stir in the butter to obtain a salted butter caramel. Add the apple quarters to the pan and cook gently over very low heat for 5 minutes. Arrange the apples neatly in the pan and let cool.

Roll out the pastry in a circle larger than the diameter of the pan and lay it on top of the fruit, tucking in the edges down between the fruit and the pan sides.

Bake until golden, 25–30 minutes.

Remove from the oven and let stand for 5 minutes. Turn the tarte Tatin out of the pan by placing the serving plate face down on the pie crust lid and, while holding it firmly in place, quickly turn the pan over.

If any of the apple pieces stay attached to the pan after you've flipped it out, simply remove them from the pan and stick them back in place like a jigsaw puzzle, scraping the pan well to remove all bits of caramel.

Serve with one of the ice creams or accompaniments suggested on page 40.

MILK CHOCOLATE, SPICED COOKIES, AND BUTTERSCOTCH CAKE

Serves 8–10
Preparation time: 20 minutes
Cooking time: 10 minutes
Refrigeration time: 2 hours

4–5 oz (125–150 g) spice-flavored cookies (ginger, cinnamon, cloves, nutmeg ...), crushed
4 dried figs, finely chopped
4 large juicy dates, finely chopped
2 Tbsp (30 mL) golden raisins
1/4 cup plus 1 Tbsp (60 mL) salted butter, melted
2/3 cup (150 mL) whipping cream
7 oz (200 g) milk chocolate, broken into pieces
2 packs caramel candies (Werthers Originals would be good)

In a bowl, combine the crushed biscuits, figs, dates, golden raisins, and butter. Press this mixture into the base of an 8-inch (2-L) cake pan. Refrigerate until hardened.

Bring the cream just to a boil in a saucepan. Put the chocolate pieces in a bowl, pour over the hot cream and stir until smooth. Pour the chocolate cream over the crushed biscuit base and refrigerate to harden for 2 hours.

Just before serving, put the caramel candies in a tea towel and crush with a rolling pin. Sprinkle the crushed candies over the cake and serve.

CARAMEL IN ANY LANGUAGE

TREACLE TART

IN SPITE OF ITS NAME, THIS TART IS MADE WITH "GOLDEN SYRUP," A BRITISH
PRODUCT YOU MAY BE ABLE TO FIND IN SPECIALTY STORES, BUT, IF NOT, USE
CORN OR MAPLE SYRUP. TREACLE TART IS A CLASSIC DESSERT IN AN AGE-OLD
TRADITION OF COMFORT FOOD.

Serves 6
Preparation time: 25 minutes
Chilling time: 1¹/₂ hours
Cooking time: 30 minutes

For the pastry
¹/₃ cup (75 mL) chilled butter, cut into cubes
1¹/₄ cups (300 mL) all-purpose flour
2 Tbsp (30 mL) soft brown sugar
1 Tbsp (15 mL) chilled water

For the filling
²/₃ cup (150 mL) Golden Syrup (corn or maple syrup)
1¹/₂ Tbsp (20 mL) butter
¹/₃ cup (75 mL) whipping cream
2 eggs, lightly beaten

To make the pasty, mix the butter, flour, and sugar together in a food processor, or in
a mixing bowl, using your fingertips to combine, until the mixture resembles coarse
breadcrumbs. Make a hollow in the center and pour in sufficient chilled water to make
a dough. Shape into a ball, cover with plastic wrap, and chill in the refrigerator for
1 hour.

Roll out the pastry and use it to line a 9-inch (23-cm) round loose-bottomed flan pan.
Chill in the refrigerator for a further 30 minutes.

Preheat the oven to 350°F (180°C) and put a baking sheet in the oven to heat up.

Gently heat the Golden Syrup in a small saucepan. Add the butter and stir until the
mixture is smooth. Remove the pan from the heat and gently stir in the cream and
beaten eggs.

Pour the filling into the pie shell and bake for 30–35 minutes until the crust is golden
brown and the filling has set.

Allow the tart to cool for a few minutes before serving.

CARAMEL BUTTER CREAM AND MAPLE SYRUP LAYER CAKE

Serves 10–12
Preparation time: 25 minutes
Cooking time: 30 minutes

For the cake
3¹/₂ cups (875 mL) all-purpose flour
1¹/₂ cups less 2 Tbsp (300 mL) soft brown sugar
1 cup plus 2 Tbsp (250 mL) white superfine sugar
8 eggs
2 cups (500 mL) salted butter, softened
2 Tbsp (30 mL) baking powder

For the caramel butter cream
1 lb (500 g) icing (confectioner's) sugar
1 cup (250 mL) butter, softened
2–3 Tbsp (30–45 mL) liquid caramel (store-bought)
1–2 Tbsp (15–30 mL) mascarpone

For the caramelized hazelnuts (praline, see page 36)
³/₄ cup (75 g) hazelnuts, shelled and toasted (in the oven or in a skillet)
2 Tbsp (30 mL) water
¹/₂ cup less 1 Tbsp (100 mL) granulated sugar
¹/₃ cup (75 mL) maple syrup

Preheat the oven to 350°F (180°C).

Grease and flour two 9-inch (1.5-L) sponge pans. Put all the cake ingredients in the bowl of a food mixer and mix to obtain a smooth, even texture.

Divide the mixture equally between the sponge pans, smooth with a palette knife, and bake in the oven for 30 minutes or until the surface of the cakes is golden brown. Check they are cooked through by inserting the blade of a knife into the center—it should come out clean.

Remove the cakes from the oven and leave to stand for a few minutes before turning them out of the pans and leaving to cool completely on a wire rack.

When completely cool, cut each cake in half horizontally to obtain 4 rounds.

To make the butter cream, beat the icing sugar and softened butter until the mixture is smooth. Add the liquid caramel and mascarpone to slacken and froth up the butter cream. Allow to set in the refrigerator for a few minutes, if necessary, then spread a layer of butter cream on each of 3 cake rounds, reserving a larger portion for the topping. Place the rounds one on top of the other adding the extra portion of butter cream to the top layer and leave to set.

Spread the hazelnuts on a silicone liner or parchment paper. Make a caramel with the water and sugar (see page 12), pour over the hazelnuts, and leave to set. Break the caramelized hazelnut praline into pieces and use them to decorate the top of the cake.

Just before serving, drizzle the maple syrup over cake and let it run down the sides.

CRÊPES SUZETTE

RATHER LIKE "TARTE TATIN," CRÊPES SUZETTE WERE INVENTED BY A CLUMSY COOK WHO ACCIDENTALLY FLAMBÉED HIS CRÊPES WHEN HE SPILT COGNAC OVER THEM. YOU DON'T HAVE TO FLAMBÉ THE CRÊPES, THE IMPORTANT THING IS TO LET THEM SOAK UP THE DELICIOUS CARAMELIZED ORANGE SYRUP IN THE BOTTOM OF THE PAN.

Serves 4
Preparation time: 10 minutes
Resting time for the crêpe batter: 1 hour
Cooking time for the crêpes: 15 minutes
Cooking time for the crêpes and sauce: 15 minutes

For the crêpes
1 cup (250 mL) all-purpose flour
1 Tbsp (15 mL) sugar
2 medium eggs, beaten
1 cup (250 mL) whole milk
Grated rind of 2 oranges

For the syrup
1/2 cup less 1 Tbsp (100 mL) granulated sugar
4 Tbsp lemon juice
4 Tbsp orange juice
1/2 cup (125 mL) butter

Vanilla ice cream, to serve

To make the crêpes, sift the flour into a large mixing bowl and add the sugar. Make a hollow in the center and gradually incorporate the beaten eggs, milk, and orange grated rind. Beat until you have a smooth, light mixture with no lumps. Leave to rest for 1 hour.

Melt a little butter in a skillet and cook the crêpes one at a time. Turn onto a plate, keeping them flat, and keep warm. The mixture should make 8 small crêpes.

To make the syrup, add the sugar to the skillet and caramelize. Stir in the lemon and orange juice, and allow to reduce slightly. Add the butter, stirring well to dissolve any sugar crystals that may have formed in the pan.

Place the crêpes one at a time in the skillet, keeping them flat, and then fold them as they soak up the syrup.

Serve immediately, possibly with a scoop of vanilla ice cream.

HONEY-COATED FLAPJACKS

Makes 1 dozen flapjacks
Preparation time: 15 minutes
Cooking time: 25 minutes

1 cup (250 mL) salted butter
3/4 cup (175 mL) Golden Syrup (corn or maple syrup)
1 cup (250 mL) granulated sugar
3 3/4 cups (425 g) rolled oats
2 Tbsp (30 mL) slivered almonds
1/4 cup (50 mL) honey

Preheat the oven to 350°F (180°C).

Heat the butter, syrup, and sugar together in a saucepan, stirring with a wooden spoon until the butter melts. Remove from the heat, add the rolled oats and almonds, and mix well.

Pour the mixture into a greased 8-inch (2-L) square baking pan, spread evenly, and bake in the oven for 25 minutes. The center should still be slightly soft, as the flapjacks will harden as they cool.

Remove from the oven and leave until almost completely cool. Spread the honey over the top of the flapjacks and cut into squares.

CARAMELIZED BREAD AND BUTTER PUDDING

Serves 8
Preparation time: 10 minutes
Resting time: 20 minutes
Cooking time: 40–50 minutes

6–7 slices white bread, from a sandwich loaf
2 cups (500 mL) whole milk
2 cups (500 mL) whipping cream
1 vanilla bean, split in half lengthwise, seeds scraped out and set aside
3 egg yolks
1/4 cup (50 mL) soft brown sugar

Cut the slices of bread into triangles and arrange in an ovenproof dish.

Bring the milk and cream to a boil together with the vanilla bean and its seeds.

Meanwhile, beat the egg yolks and sugar until the mixture turns light and pale yellow in color, and doubles in volume.

Remove the vanilla bean and pour the hot milk and cream onto the eggs and sugar while whisking continuously. Pour this mixture onto the bread and leave to swell for 15 minutes.

Preheat the oven to 325°F (160°C).

Place the dish in the oven and bake for 40 minutes.

Just before serving, sprinkle with the sugar and caramelize with a kitchen blow torch, or quickly under a preheated broiler.

Serve with crème fraîche or a sorbet (see page 40).

DARK CHOCOLATE AND CARAMEL NUT TART

Serves 8
Preparation time: 30 minutes
Cooking time: 40 minutes
Chilling time for the pastry: $1\frac{1}{2}$ hours in total
Chilling time for the tart: 3–4 hours

For the pastry
$\frac{1}{2}$ cup (125 mL) salted butter, chilled and cut in cubes
$1\frac{1}{4}$ cups (325 mL) all-purpose flour
$\frac{1}{4}$ cup (50 mL) soft brown sugar
$\frac{3}{4}$ cup (75 g) hazelnuts, chopped and toasted
1 Tbsp (15 mL) chilled water

For the filling
1 cup less 2 Tbsp (200 mL) granulated sugar
2 Tbsp (30 mL) water
$1\frac{1}{2}$ cups (350 mL) whipping cream
$\frac{1}{4}$ cup (50 mL) butter
3 eggs, lightly beaten
$\frac{1}{2}$ lb (250 g) hazelnuts, shelled and toasted, or toasted pine nuts

For the topping
$3\frac{1}{4}$ cups (800 mL) whipping cream
5 oz (150 g) dark chocolate, broken in pieces

To prepare the pastry, put all the ingredients (apart from the water) in the bowl of a food processor, or a large mixing bowl using your fingertips to combine, and mix to obtain a fine crumbly texture. Add sufficient of the chilled water to bind the mixture, shape into a ball, and chill in the refrigerator for about 1 hour.

Roll out the pastry and use it to line the base and sides of a 9-inch (23-cm) round flan pan, pressing in place firmly to prevent trapping any air bubbles, prick all over with a fork, and chill for a further 30 minutes.

Preheat the oven to 400°F (200°C) and put a baking sheet on the shelf to heat up.

Place the pastry shell in the oven on the baking sheet and bake for 15 minutes. Remove from the oven and reduce the temperature to 350°F (180°C).

For the filling, make a caramel with the sugar and water (see page 12). Remove from the heat, add the cream and return to the heat for 5 minutes, stirring continuously. Add the butter, mix well, and leave to cool for 10 minutes. Finally, add the beaten eggs and mix in well.

Arrange the toasted hazelnuts or pine nuts on the tart base, cover with the caramel filling, and bake in the oven for 20 minutes. The caramel should still be very soft in the center of the tart and slightly set around the edges.

Remove from the oven and leave to cool.

To make the topping, melt the cream and chocolate together in a heatproof bowl set over a saucepan of barely simmering water, or in a microwave oven, following the maker's instructions. Stir well so that the topping is smooth, then spread it over the surface of the cooled tart.

Chill in the refrigerator for 3–4 hours before serving.

As this tart is made in several stages, it's a good idea to make it the day before you want to serve it. If you're really short of time, you can always blind bake the pastry shell as described in the TIP on page 82 (ready-made pastry is not an option for this recipe!), fill with the cold Salted Butter Caramel Sauce on page 30, and top with the chocolate cream.

STICKY TOFFEE PUDDING

THIS DESSERT WAS FIRST FEATURED IN A BRITISH TELEVISION COOKERY
PROGRAM AROUND 1990 AND IT IMMEDIATELY BECAME A "MUST" AT ALL DINNER
PARTIES. THERE ARE SEVERAL VERSIONS AND IT'S STILL A VERY POPULAR
DESSERT (SOME WOULD EVEN SAY "CULT") IN RESTAURANTS,
BRITISH "PUBS," AND EVERYWHERE WHERE PEOPLE STILL HAVE ROOM FOR
A "PROPER PUDDING" AT THE END OF THE MEAL.

Makes 6 small puddings
Preparation time: 15 minutes
Cooking time: 20–25 minutes

$^1/_4$ cup plus tsp (60 mL) butter, softened
1 cup (250 mL) soft brown sugar or demerara sugar
3 Tbsp (45 mL) Golden Syrup (corn or maple syrup)
2 eggs
$1^1/_2$ cups (375 mL) all-purpose flour
2 tsp (10 mL) baking powder
$1^1/_4$ cups (300 mL) boiling water
7 oz (200 g) pitted dates
1 Tsp baking soda
$^1/_2$ tsp (2 mL) vanilla extract

For the sauce
$^1/_2$ cup less 1 Tbsp (110 mL) heavy whipping cream
$^1/_4$ cup plus 1 Tbsp (60 mL) butter, cut in cubes
$^1/_2$ cup packed (60 mL) dark muscovado sugar
3 Tbsp (45 nL) Golden Syrup (or corn syrup)

Grease and flour 6 small metal pudding moulds or dariole moulds.

Preheat the oven to 400°F (200°C).

Beat the softened butter and sugar together in a food mixer or by hand with a balloon
whisk until it's pale, light, and fluffy. Carefully add the Golden Syrup or corn syrup and
eggs, while still beating, until you obtain a smooth texture. Sift together the flour and
baking powder and add gently, in 2 or 3 stages, with a metal spoon.

Pour the boiling water into a blender, add the dates and reduce to a purée. Add the
baking soda and vanilla extract. Stir the warm date purée into the pudding batter
and mix well.

Fill the moulds with the mixture, stand them on a baking sheet and bake in the oven
for 20–25 minutes until the surface of the puddings is firm.

To make the sauce, put all the ingredients in a saucepan and bring slowly to a boil,
stirring frequently.

Turn the puddings out of their moulds onto dessert dishes, cover with the sauce, and
serve with ice cream (see page 40), whipped cream, or crème fraîche.

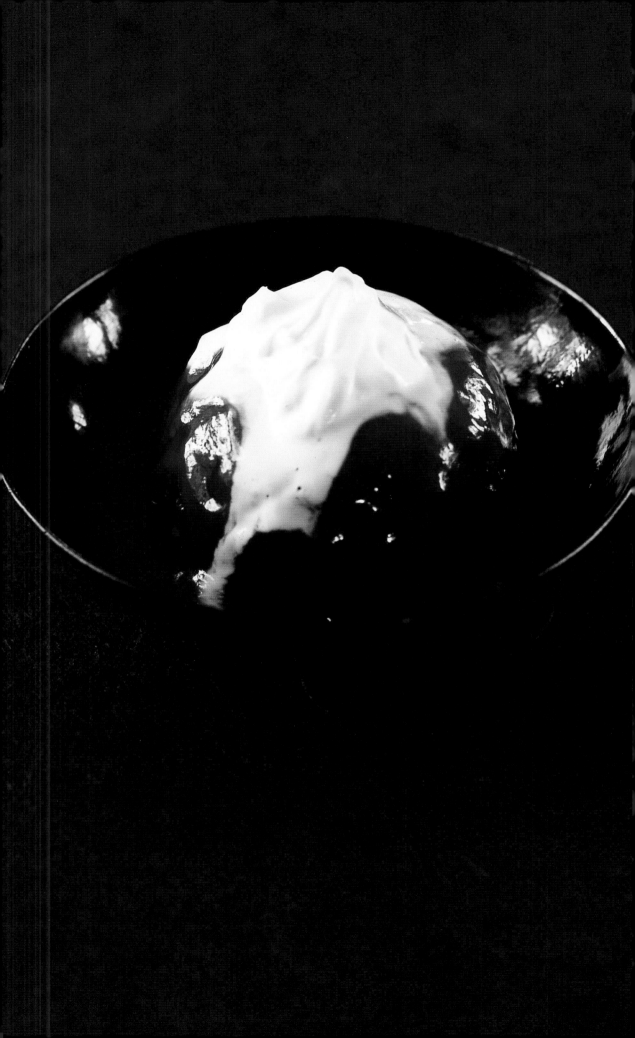

GOLDEN SYRUP CAKE, WITH GOLDEN SYRUP AND LEMON BUTTER

THIS CAKE IS SOMETHING OF A BRITISH INSTITUTION—SOFT AND SWEET, IT SEEMS TO BE INFUSED WITH DELICIOUS "GOLDEN SYRUP." SERVE WITH A GOOD-QUALITY TEA, ON SUNDAY AT ABOUT 5 O'CLOCK, SLICED, LIGHTLY TOASTED UNDER THE BROILER, AND SPREAD WITH THIS BUTTER—IT WILL LITERALLY MELT IN YOUR MOUTH.

Serves 6
Preparation time: 5 minutes
Cooking time: about 1 minute per slice

1 Golden Syrup cake or a gingerbread cake

For the butter
$^1/_2$ cup less 1 Tbsp (100 mL) best-quality salted butter, softened
1 Tbsp (15 mL) soft brown sugar
Grated rind of 1 lemon
1 Tbsp (15 mL) Golden Syrup or corn syrup

Mix the softened butter with the sugar and lemon grated rind.

Add the syrup, leaving golden streaks in the butter.

To serve, spread on slices of cake, cold or lightly toasted under a broiler—don't use the toaster!

CARAMELIZED RICE PUDDING, FLAVORED WITH PRUNES AND GRAND MARNIER

Serves 4–6
30–35 minutes cooking time

2 cups (500 mL) milk
2 cups (500 mL) whipping cream
1/4 cup (50 mL) granulated sugar
1 vanilla bean, split in half lengthwise, seeds scraped
   out and set aside
1 cup (200 g) short-grain (pudding) rice
3–4 Tbsp prune purée
1 Tbsp (15 mL) Grand Marnier
2 Tbsp (30 mL) mascarpone (optional)

To caramelize
1/2 cup less 1 Tbsp (100 mL) granulated sugar

Bring the milk and cream just to a boil with the sugar, vanilla bean, and its seeds.

Add the rice as the milk is just beginning to boil and cook over a low heat for 30–40 minutes, stirring occasionally to keep it from catching. If the rice does begin to catch, stir in a little more milk.

Stir the Grand Marnier into the prune purée and pour the mixture into a serving dish or individual dessert bowls.

Remove the vanilla bean, mix in the mascarpone if you want the rice to be extra creamy, and pour the rice onto the prune purée. Leave to cool a little before sprinkling with sugar and caramelizing with a kitchen blow torch, or under a preheated broiler.

Serve hot, warm, or chilled.

BANOFFEE PIE

ONE OF THE MOST EXQUISITE CARAMELIZED COMBINATIONS—TOFFEE, BANANAS, CREAM, AND A HINT OF SALT ON A CRISP, CRUNCHY BASE. A GREAT CLASSIC THAT'S IN A LEAGUE OF ITS OWN.

Serves 6–8
Preparation time: 20 minutes
Cooking time: microwave 15 minutes;
double boiler 40–50 minutes
Chilling time: 2–3 hours

1 x 14 oz can sweetened condensed milk
5 oz (150 g) graham crackers, crushed
1/3 cup (75 mL) salted butter, melted
3 bananas, sliced in rounds
2 Tbsp (30 mL) mascarpone
1 1/4 cups (300 mL) whipping cream, whipped
1 Tbsp (15 mL) cocoa powder

To prepare the caramel, first cook the condensed milk by one of the methods given on page 46. Set aside to cool.

Put the crushed graham crackers in a mixing bowl, add the melted butter, and mix well together. Line the base of an 8-inch (20-cm) flan pan with a removable bottom with the graham cracker crumb mixture and press well down. Leave to set in the refrigerator.

Stir the marscapone into the whipped cream. Arrange the banana rounds on the crumb base, spread with the cooled caramel, and cover with whipped cream and mascarpone mixture.

Chill in the refrigerator for 2–3 hours and then sift over a layer of cocoa powder.

Remove from the flan pan to serve.

PANNA COTTA WITH RASPBERRY CARAMEL COULIS

PANNA COTTA MEANS, LITERALLY, "COOKED CREAM." USE YOUR MOST ATTRACTIVE GLASS DESSERT DISHES TO DISPLAY THE CONTRASTING COLORS OF THIS LIGHT, DELICIOUS DESSERT.

Serves 4
Cooking time: 25 minutes
Chilling time: 4 hours minimum, preferably overnight

2 cups (500 mL) whipping cream
1/4 cup (50 mL) granulated sugar
1 vanilla bean, split in half lengthwise, seeds scraped out
2 sheets gelatin, soaked in a bowl of cold water
    (powdered gelatin: use half an 11-g sachet and follow
    maker's instructions for dissolving)
1/2 cup less 1 Tbsp (100 g) granulated sugar
2 Tbsp (30 mL) water
1/2 lb (250 g) fresh raspberries

Put the cream, 1/4 cup sugar, and the vanilla bean with its seeds into a saucepan and bring just to a boil. Simmer gently over a low heat for 15 minutes.

Take the saucepan from the heat and remove the vanilla bean. Squeeze the water from the gelatin sheets and add to the hot cream, stirring until they have completely dissolved. (If using powdered gelatin, add the completely dissolved crystals to the pan and stir in thoroughly.)

Pour the cream into individual dessert dishes and chill in the refrigerator for at least 4 hours to set or, if possible, overnight.

Make a caramel with the sugar and water (see page 12). Remove from the heat, add the whole raspberries, and return the saucepan to the heat to dissolve any sugar crystals that may have formed. Leave until completely cool, then pour a layer of the raspberry caramel over each panna cotta and chill until ready to serve.

COUPE MELBA

A VARIATION ON A CLASSIC COMBINATION THAT'S A REAL WINNER. IN THIS VERSION, THE CARAMELIZATION ADDS THE FINISHING TOUCH TO THIS EXTREMELY SIMPLE COOKED DESSERT, WHICH IS SERVED COLD.

Serves 4
Preparation time: 10 minutes
Cooking time: 10 minutes
Chilling time: 1 hour for the raspberry sauce

1/2 lb (250 g) fresh raspberries or strawberries
2 Tbsp (30 mL) icing (confectioner's) sugar
1/4 cup (50 ml) salted butter
2 yellow nectarines, peeled if preferred
2 Tbsp (30 mL) soft brown sugar
4 scoops best-quality vanilla ice cream (see page 40),
    or mascarpone mousse (see page 74)

To prepare the raspberry sauce, cook the fruit in a small saucepan with a little water. Reduce to a purée and add the icing sugar. Leave to cool.

Strawberries will lose their flavor if pre-cooked, so simply hull and reduce to a purée with the icing sugar and leave to cool.

Heat the butter in a skillet, cut the nectarines in half, discard the pit, and place in the skillet. After cooking gently for 1–2 minutes, add the sugar and then spoon the sauce formed by the fruit juices, butter, and sugar over the nectarines, making sure the caramel doesn't burn. Put to one side.

Put a scoop of ice cream into each of 4 attractive glass dessert dishes, drizzle with raspberry or strawberry sauce, top with a caramelized nectarine half, and serve.

DARK CHOCOLATE COUSCOUS WITH RASPBERRY CARAMEL

Serves 6
Cooking time: 20 minutes

4 sugar lumps for the caramel
1 cup (5–6 oz) fresh raspberries
2/3 lb (350 g) couscous
6 oz (175 g) best-quality dark chocolate, broken into
    small pieces, plus a bit extra
2 Tbsp (30 mL) sugar

Make a caramel with the sugar lumps soaked in a little water (see page 12). Remove from the heat and add 3/4 of the raspberries, taking care not to splash yourself with the caramel.

The raspberries will cook in the hot caramel, releasing their juice, which will blend deliciously with the caramel. If sugar crystals form, return the pan to the heat and heat gently.

Strain the juice through a sieve and add the rest of the raspberries, but don't stir too much, so that they poach a little in the juice while remaining whole. Put to one side.

Overcook the couscous—it's easy to do, just ignore the cooking instructions on the packet. When it's all swollen and sticky, add the chocolate pieces and stir in thoroughly so that they melt into the grains. (You may need a bit more chocolate and if you don't, then all the more to nibble at while you're cooking!) Add the sugar and stir again.

Serve the warm chocolate couscous in individual dessert dishes. Make a hollow in the center and pour in the raspberry caramel.

BUTTERSCOTCH DELIGHTS WITH APPLESAUCE, FUDGE, AND SHORTBREAD

WHEN I WAS A LITTLE GIRL, WE HAD A TYPE OF JELL-O INSTANT PUDDING KNOWN AS "ANGEL DELIGHT." IT CAME IN ALL KINDS OF FLAVORS, BUT TODAY, THE ONLY ONE THAT'S OF ANY REAL INTEREST TO ME (APART FROM THOSE PROVIDING A LITTLE NOSTALGIC PLEASURE) IS THE "BUTTERSCOTCH." COMBINED WITH A QUALITY SCOTCH SHORTBREAD COOKIE MADE WITH BUTTER AND DEMERARA SUGAR, A SPOONFUL OF APPLESAUCE, AND A PIECE OF FUDGE, IT CREATES A BLEND OF FLAVORS THAT'S TOTALLY CONTRIVED, BUT UTTERLY IRRESISTIBLE.

Makes 6 shortbreads
Preparation time: 5 minutes
Chilling time: about 10 minutes

1 packet Jell-O Instant Pudding, butterscotch flavor
1 cup (250 mL) 2% milk
5 oz (150 g) ready-made applesauce
6 quality round Scotch shortbread cookies, found in specialty stores
6 small pieces fudge

Follow the instructions on the packet of Jell-O Instant Pudding—whisk into the chilled milk and leave to set. Put a spoonful of applesauce onto a round of shortbread, top with a spoonful of Jell-O Instant Pudding, and decorate with a small piece of fudge—it couldn't be easier.

LITTLE POTS OF CARAMEL

Serves 6
Preparation time: 10 minutes
Cooking time: 50 minutes

^{2}/$_3$ cup (150 mL) sugar
2 Tbsp (30 mL) water
1^1/$_4$ cups (300 mL) whipping cream
2 cups (500 mL) whole milk
1 vanilla bean, split in half lengthwise, seeds scraped out and set aside
4 egg yolks
^{1}/$_4$ cup plus 1 Tbsp (60 g) granulated sugar

Make a caramel with the sugar and water (see page 12). Leave to cool slightly before pouring into the bottom of 6 small ovenproof pots or ramekins.

Put the cream, milk, and vanilla bean with its seeds in a saucepan and bring slowly just to a boil. Remove the vanilla bean.

Meanwhile beat the egg yolks and sugar together in a large mixing bowl until the mixture lightens in color and doubles in volume. Pour the hot milk and cream onto the beaten egg yolks and mix well.

Divide the mixture between the pots or ramekins, leaving a little space at the top, and place in a steamer, cover, and leave to cook for 45 minutes. Allow to cool completely before serving.

CRÈME BRÛLÉE

THIS SIMPLE DESSERT, IRRESISTIBLY CREAMY UNDER ITS CRISP CARAMEL TOPPING, HAS BECOME AN ALL-TIME FAVORITE IN MANY COUNTRIES. AS A RESULT, IT'S BEEN THE SUBJECT OF SOME DUBIOUS EXPERIMENTS IN SWEET-AND-SAVORY COMBINATIONS THAT HAVE NOT ALWAYS BEEN A SUCCESS. HERE IT IS IN ITS SIMPLEST FORM.

Makes 4 crèmes brûlées
Preparation time: 20 minutes
Cooking time: 15 minutes
Chilling time: 4–5 hours

2^1/$_2$ cups (625 mL) whipping cream
1 vanilla bean, split in half lengthwise, seeds scraped out and set aside
6 egg yolks
2 Tbsp (30 mL) superfine sugar

For the caramel topping
^{1}/$_3$ cup plus 1 Tbsp (90 mL) sugar, brown or white

Preheat the oven to 375°F (190°C) and put a baking sheet on the shelf to heat up.

Heat the cream, vanilla bean, and its seeds in a saucepan, not quite to a boil. Beat the egg yolks and superfine sugar together in a large mixing bowl until the mixture turns light and pale yellow in color and doubles in volume.

Remove the vanilla bean and mix to ensure that the seeds are well dispersed in the warm cream. Pour onto the beaten egg yolks and mix well.

Put 4 small ovenproof dishes or ramekins in a roasting pan—or any other large ovenproof dish—and fill the dishes with the cream mixture. Place the roasting pan on the hot baking sheet in the oven, then pull the shelf of the oven out a little way. Pour boiling water into the roasting pan about half way up the sides of the dishes, then gently slide the shelf back into the oven and bake for about 15 minutes. A thin skin will form on the surface of the creams.

Remove from the oven, leave to cool, and then chill in the refrigerator for at least 4–5 hours, overnight if possible.

To caramelize the surface of the creams, sprinkle a layer of the sugar and place under a very hot broiler, or, better still, use a kitchen blow torch. You can serve immediately or leave to chill, it's your choice. Personally, I prefer them chilled.

VARIATIONS

These are endless, so give free rein to your imagination. Add raspberries or blueberries, chocolate, hazelnut crunch, liqueurs—in fact, any flavors you like. My favorite version came from a Viennese cabdriver who adds chopped nuts to the soft brown sugar used for the caramel, and a little coffee liqueur to the cream.

SWEET 'N' SAVORY

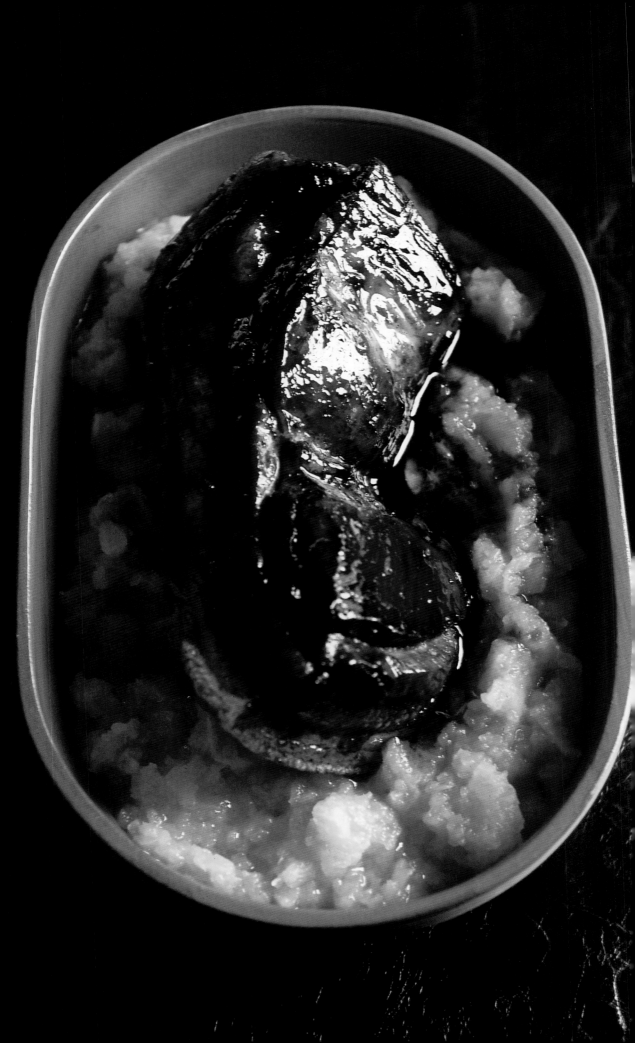

CARAMELIZED BREAST OF PORK WITH TURNIP AND PUMPKIN MASH

Serves 6
Cooking time: 2 hours
Preparation time: 20 minutes

For the pork
3 Tbsp (45 mL) olive oil
2 Tbsp (30 mL) honey
Salt and pepper
3 lb (1.5 kg) breast of pork, or pork belly

For the mash
1 lb (500 g) Gold Ball turnips, peeled
1 lb (500 g) pumpkin, peeled and diced
1/4 cup (50 mL) butter
1 Tbsp (15 mL) cumin seeds, toasted (in a dry skillet or saucepan)
Sea salt and freshly ground black pepper

Preheat the oven to 400°F (200°C).

Mix the oil with the honey, and season with salt and pepper. Coat the pork with the mixture and put in the oven, immediately lowering the temperature to 275°F (140°C).

Cook the meat for about 2 hours, basting frequently with the cooking juices.

Steam the turnips and pumpkin separately, in a steamer. When the vegetables are nice and tender, mash together with the butter and cumin seeds. Season to taste with sea salt and freshly ground black pepper.

Slice the pork, season with salt and pepper, and serve with the pumpkin and turnip mash.

CHINATOWN QUAIL

Serves 4
Cooking time: 20 minutes
Cooking time: 30 minutes

3 Tbsp (45 mL) honey
2 Tbsp (30 mL) light soy sauce
Sea salt and freshly ground black pepper
4 quails
Olive oil

Mix the honey and soy sauce in a roasting pan and season with salt and pepper. Add the quails to the marinade for 30–40 minutes, turning from time to time.

Preheat the oven to 400°F (200°C).

Drizzle a little olive oil over the quails and roast in the oven for 20–25 minutes, basting frequently with the honey and soy sauce marinade to create a delicious glaze.

Remove from the oven and serve immediately with a crisp salad.

PORK TENDERLOIN IN ORANGE CARAMEL SAUCE

Serves 3–4
Preparation time: 10 minutes
Cooking time: 20 minutes

1/4 cup plus 1 Tbsp (60 mL) light soy sauce
1/2 cup (125 mL) sugar
1 Tbsp (15 mL) fresh ginger, grated
1 garlic clove, crushed
1 Tbsp (15 mL) Thai fish sauce (Nam Pla)
2 Tbsp (30 mL) lime juice
Grated rind from 2 oranges and 4 Tbsp of the juice
1 lb (500 g) tenderloin of pork, cut in half lengthwise

Put all the ingredients except the meat in a skillet, place over moderate heat, and stir until the sauce thickens. Add the pork to the skillet and cook, turning frequently, and basting continuously with the sauce.

When the meat is well glazed, and a thin skewer passes easily through the meat, remove from the skillet. Let rest for a few moments before cutting into slices. Drizzle with the thick and deliciously sticky sauce, and serve with a crisp salad or lightly cooked snow peas or sugar snap peas.

ROAST PHEASANT WITH CARAMELIZED APPLES

A REALLY SIMPLE RECIPE—JUST REMEMBER TO LEAVE THE PHEASANT TO STAND FOR A WHILE BEFORE YOU CARVE.

Serves 4
Preparation time: 10 minutes
Cooking time: 40 minutes

For the pheasant
1 prepared pheasant, about 2 lb (1 kg)
1 shallot, peeled
2 Tbsp (30 mL) olive oil
Salt and freshly ground black pepper

For the caramelized apples
1/4 cup plus 1 Tbsp (65 g) salted butter
1 shallot, peeled and finely chopped
8 apples (Golden Delicious, McIntosh ...) peeled and
   cut in quarters
2 Tbsp (30 mL) soft brown sugar

Preheat the oven to 425°F (220°C).

Put the pheasant in a roasting pan, rub the skin with the shallot and then place it in the body cavity. Drizzle the pheasant with a little olive oil.

Roast in the oven for 15 minutes, then lower the temperature to 350°F (180°C) and cook for another 20 minutes or so. When the bird is pierced between the breast and leg, the juice should be clear.

Leave the pheasant to stand for a good 10 minutes. Cut into portions and keep warm.

Pour the cooking juices from the roasting pan into a saucepan and skim off the fat. Add a little boiling water to the pan, scrape the bottom well, and add to the cooking juices. Reduce, season with salt and pepper, and keep to one side.

Heat the butter in a separate skillet and fry the chopped shallot lightly without letting it brown. Add the apples and brown on all sides. Add the sugar and caramelize the apples.

Serve the pheasant with the caramelized apples and cooking juices.

OSTRICH MEDALLIONS AND CARAMELIZED PLUMS WITH WINE VINEGAR

THE PLUMS GO JUST AS WELL WITH VENISON, WILD BOAR, AND OTHER GAME MEATS. OSTRICH, WITH ITS DISTINCTIVE FLAVOR, HAS THE ADVANTAGE OF BEING AVAILABLE FOR MOST OF THE YEAR IN SUPERMARKETS.

Serves 4
Preparation time: 5 minutes
Cooking time: 10 minutes

2 Tbsp (30 mL) peanut or vegetable oil
4 ostrich medallions, each 1/4 lb (125 g)
1/4 cup (50 mL) butter
1 shallot, peeled and finely chopped
1 dozen newly ripened red plums, halved and pitted
2 Tbsp (30 mL) soft brown sugar
2 Tbsp (30 mL) red wine vinegar
Salt and freshly ground black pepper

Heat 1 Tbsp peanut oil in a skillet and brown the medallions over moderate heat. Remove from the skillet, and keep warm. Add the butter, shallot, and then the plums.

Brown for a few minutes before adding the sugar. Caramelize the plums, remove from the skillet, and keep warm with the ostrich. Deglaze the skillet with the wine vinegar. Drizzle the sauce over the meat and plums, and serve.

PIZZA WITH SMOKED CHICKEN, CARAMELIZED PINEAPPLE, AND MOZZARELLA CHEESE

Serves 4
Preparation time: 10 minutes
Cooking time: 20 minutes

2 Tbsp (30 mL) salted butter
1/2 fresh pineapple, peeled and cut in segments
2 Tbsp (30 mL) granulated sugar
1 ready-made pizza base
1/2 lb (250 g) mozzarella cheese made with buffalo's milk,
   drained and diced
1/4 cup (50 mL) tomato paste
5 oz (150 g) smoked chicken, cut into thin strips

Preheat the oven to 425°F (220°C).

Heat the butter in a skillet. Pan-fry the pineapple segments and then caramelize by adding the sugar while they are cooking, and turning regularly. Set aside and keep warm.

Place the pizza base on a greased baking sheet. Use the back of a spoon to spread the tomato paste on the pizza base and top with alternate pieces of chicken, pineapple, and mozzarella cheese.

Bake in the oven for about 20 minutes, but check now and again to see the caramelized pineapple is not getting burnt.

CARAMELIZED SALMON

Serves 4
Preparation time: 10 minutes
Cooking time: 10 minutes

½ cup less 1 Tbsp (100 g) soft light brown sugar
½ cup (125 mL) water
1 thumb-sized piece fresh ginger, peeled and grated
2 garlic cloves, peeled and finely chopped
4 Tbsp Thai fish sauce (Nam Pla)
Grated rind of 1 lime
2 Tbsp (30 mL) lime juice
Grated rind of 1 orange
2 Tbsp (30 mL) orange juice
12 oz (350 g) salmon fillet, cut in ¾-inch (2-cm) cubes

Put all the ingredients except the salmon in a saucepan and cook for 3–4 minutes, stirring, to reduce the sauce.

Heat a large skillet and pan-fry the salmon with the sauce for just a few minutes, stirring continuously. The salmon should remain pink while the sauce turns thick and syrupy, but take care not to let it burn.

Serve immediately with Thai rice (jasmine rice) and a crisp salad.

You can also stir-fry the fish in a wok with crunchy vegetables.

BOK CHOY AND PEANUT SPROUTS WITH PEANUT OIL AND SOY SAUCE

ALL RIGHT, SO THESE MAY NOT BE EVERYDAY INGREDIENTS THAT YOU CAN PICK UP WHERE YOU NORMALLY DO YOUR GROCERY SHOPPING—YOU'LL PROBABLY HAVE TO GO TO CHINATOWN OR A SPECIALIST STORE TO TRACK THEM DOWN. HOWEVER, THERE ARE OFTEN NEW FOOD PRODUCTS IN EVEN THE MOST BASIC SECTIONS OF OUR SUPERMARKETS—PACKS OF MIXED SALAD OR STIR-FRY VEGETABLES THAT YOU CAN TRY BEFORE GOING IN SEARCH OF THE REAL MCCOY AMONG THE FRUIT AND VEG ON YOUR LOCAL MARKET STALLS.

Serves 6
Preparation time: 15 minutes
Cooking time: 5 minutes

3 heads bok choy, cut in pieces
4–5 handfuls peanut sprouts
3–4 handfuls new season asparagus
2–3 handfuls garlic sprouts
1 chili pepper, finely chopped, but how hot is your choice
2–3 Tbsp (30–45 mL) peanut oil
2 Tbsp (30 mL) light soy sauce

Wash the vegetables, drain well, and pat dry with kitchen towels.

Heat the oil in a wok. When it begins to smoke, throw in the vegetables and cook rapidly, stirring continuously.

Season with soy sauce and serve immediately.

HERB SALAD

THE BEST ACCOMPANIMENT FOR CARAMELIZED MEAT AND FISH IS A SALAD BURSTING WITH FRESHNESS AND FLAVOR. COMBINE MINT AND BASIL WITH SALAD INGREDIENTS LIKE GREEN (OR LEAF) MUSTARD, ARUGULA, OR, IF YOU PREFER SOMETHING A LITTLE MILDER, CORN SALAD (MÂCHE).

MAKE A VINAIGRETTE WITHOUT MUSTARD, BUT INSTEAD WITH LIME JUICE, A NEUTRAL OIL, AND A FINELY CHOPPED CHILI PEPPER (TO TASTE) TO SPICE THINGS UP A BIT.

CRUNCHY STIR-FRY VEGETABLES

Serves 4
Preparation time: 15 minutes
Cooking time: 10 minutes

2 Tbsp (30 mL) sunflower oil
3 carrots, peeled, and cut in fine strips
3 parsnips, peeled, and cut in fine strips
2 yellow bell peppers, washed, and cut in fine strips
Garlic and chili pepper, quantity as required, finely chopped (optional)
1 dozen pink radishes, washed, and sliced
2 handfuls soybean sprouts, rinsed
2 Tbsp (30 mL) light soy sauce

Heat the oil in a wok. When it begins to smoke, throw in the carrots, parsnips, and bell peppers with the garlic and chili pepper, if using. Cook the vegetables for 3–4 minutes, stirring continuously. Add the radishes and soybean sprouts (which cook more quickly), stir for another 1–2 minutes, season with soy sauce, and serve.

TRICOLOR CAULIFLOWER SALAD WITH CARAMELIZED ALMONDS, GOLDEN RAISINS, AND HUMMUS VINAIGRETTE

Serves 6
10 minutes preparation time
25 minutes cooking time

$1/3$ white cauliflower
$1/3$ green cauliflower (Romanesco, if in season)
$1/3$ purple cauliflower
1 cup (100 g) blanched almonds
2 Tbsp (30 mL) sugar
$1/4$ cup (50 mL) golden raisins

For the vinaigrette
$1/4$ cup plus 2 Tbsp (80 mL) olive oil
2 Tbsp (30 mL) hummus
2 Tbsp (30 mL) lemon juice

Steam the 3 types of cauliflower separately—in a steamer—so that they remain slightly crunchy. Leave to cool.

Caramelize the almonds in a skillet with the sugar —no need to add butter. Mix with the golden raisins and keep to one side.

When the cauliflowers are completely cool, cut into small pieces, keeping the florets whole, and mix all three colors with the almonds and golden raisins.

Prepare a vinaigrette with the remaining ingredients, adding a little water if it's too thick.

Serve with a salad or as an accompaniment to a main course.

CARAMELIZED VEGETABLES

THIS MEANS MAKING THE MOST OF THE CARAMELIZED FLAVOR OF CERTAIN OVEN-BAKED OR ROASTED VEGETABLES. OFTEN IT'S ENOUGH TO LET THE SUGAR IN THE VEGETABLES DO ITS WORK, BUT A TOUCH OF HONEY OR SUGAR CAN SOMETIMES HELP THEM ON THEIR WAY.

CARROTS

The sweetest vegetable of all. Like tomatoes, carrots can easily be served for dessert. For a sweet-and-savory flavor, cook like parsnips.

TOMATOES

Tomatoes are so sweet that they are being served increasingly for dessert. For an exquisite cooking juice, drizzle a mixture of olive oil, sugar, and balsamic vinegar over halved tomatoes, and cook at a very low temperature—250°F (120°C)—for 2–3 hours.

If you don't have this much time, add a little olive oil and cook for 1 1/2 hours at 300°F (150°C). Cherry tomatoes take even less time to cook—barely 30 minutes—and there are some really tasty varieties widely available.

SHALLOTS

Onions, garlic, and shallots are simply bursting with sugar, so there's no need to add any when caramelizing them. Simply cook very gently in a skillet with a little oil and butter, or alongside a piece of meat roasted in the oven. Even so, a spoonful of sugar added while they're cooking will give them an irresistibly crunchy coating! (See page 152 for a few caramelized onion ideas.)

PUMPKIN

Pumpkin cooks a lot quicker than carrots and parsnips. In 30–40 minutes, depending on the size of the pieces, you'll have a fantastic accompaniment or the basis for a soup. I like to add honey and even spices like nutmeg or ground ginger.

ASPARAGUS

You won't believe how different asparagus tastes drizzled with a little olive oil and baked in an oven at 350°F (180°C) for 30 minutes.

Once you've tried it, you won't want it cooked any other way. It's just as delicious served hot, warm, or cold.

PARSNIPS

Parsnips have been around for centuries and are fast making a comeback. Prepared in much the same way as carrots, they have a flavor similar to that of turnips and a more porous texture. Drizzled with olive oil and roasted at 350°F (180°C) for about 1 hour, they are simply delicious with rare roast beef and horseradish sauce.

CARAMELIZED RATATOUILLE AND BREAD WITH GARLIC AND ROSEMARY BUTTER

Serves 4–6
Preparation time: 15 minutes
Cooking time: 30 minutes

For the ratatouille
1 eggplant, rinsed, and cut in strips
2 zucchini, rinsed, and cut in strips
1 yellow bell pepper, rinsed and cut in strips
1 red bell pepper, rinsed and cut in strips
2 cloves garlic, peeled and finely chopped
3 very ripe tomatoes, rinsed, and cut in quarters
1 red onion, peeled and cut in quarters
3–4 Tbsp (45–50 mL) olive oil
1 Tbsp (15 mL) honey
Salt and freshly ground black pepper

To serve
$\frac{1}{2}$ cup less 1 Tbsp (100 mL) salted butter, softened
1 clove garlic, peeled and chopped
1 Tbsp (15 mL) finely chopped rosemary
2 French sticks, or baguettes

Preheat the oven to 350°F (180°C).

Put all the vegetables into a baking dish.

Mix the oil and honey, and season with a little salt and pepper. Pour over the vegetables and mix with your hands until that they are well covered.

Bake in the oven for about 30 minutes, turning from time to time so that the vegetables caramelize.

Put the butter, garlic, and rosemary in a small grinder and grind to a paste.

Cut the French sticks or baguettes in half horizontally, spread one half with the garlic and rosemary butter, and put the two halves back together. Wrap in kitchen foil and put in the oven with the ratatouille for 15–20 minutes until the bread is golden brown.

Serve the ratatouille as an entrée, with the bread cut into slices, or as an accompaniment for roast meat.

FRESH PEAR, MANCHEGO CHEESE, AND ARUGULA SALAD WITH CARAMELIZED WALNUTS AND WARM WALNUT-LIQUEUR VINAIGRETTE

MANCHEGO IS A SPANISH CHEESE MADE FROM EWE'S MILK. IT'S CREAM-COLORED, FATTY, AND FIRM TO THE TOUCH. FIND IT IN SPECIALTY CHEESE STORES.

Serves 6
Preparation time: 20 minutes
Cooking time: 5 minutes

3 Tbsp (45 mL) chopped walnuts
1/2 cup less 1 Tbsp (100 mL) granulated sugar
2 Tbsp (30 mL) water
1/4 cup (50 mL) olive oil
1 Tbsp (15 mL) walnut vinegar
1 Tbsp (15 mL) walnut liqueur
Salt and freshly ground black pepper
6 ripe pears (Anjou, Bartlett, Bosc, Comice ...) peeled, cored, and thinly sliced
2 Tbsp (30 mL) lemon juice
2/3 lb (350 g) manchego cheese, shaved with a special cheese cutter or vegetable peeler
6 good handfuls arugula

Place the chopped walnuts on a silicone tray liner or parchment paper. Make a caramel with the sugar and water (see page 12) and pour over the walnuts. Leave to set.

Prepare a vinaigrette with the oil, walnut vinegar and liqueur, and season with salt and pepper.

Brush the pear slices with a little lemon juice and prepare the salad—on individual plates or on a large serving dish—by alternating the cheese, arugula, and pears.

Break the walnut caramel into small pieces and sprinkle over the salad.

Serve with the warm vinaigrette.

You can also make this salad with dried rather than fresh pears.

LEEK SOUP WITH MINT, YOGURT, AND CARAMELIZED BUTTER

A DISH INSPIRED BY A RECIPE FROM THE MORO RESTAURANT IN LONDON, WITH ITS WONDERFULLY INVENTIVE CUISINE, REDOLENT OF MEDITERRANEAN AND NORTH AFRICAN FLAVORS AND TRADITIONS.

Serves 4
Preparation time: 10 minutes
Cooking time: 30 minutes

For the soup
5 leeks, washed, drained, and finely chopped
1/4 cup (50 mL) butter
2 Tbsp (30 mL) dried mint
2 cups (500 mL) vegetable or chicken stock
2/3 lb (350 g) thick, creamy plain yogurt
Salt and freshly ground black pepper

For the caramelized butter
1/3 cup (75 mL) butter

Lightly fry the chopped leeks in the butter with 1 Tbsp dried mint, stirring regularly until they have softened. Add the stock and cook for a further 10 minutes.

Just before serving, add the yogurt and bring almost to a boil. Remove from the heat immediately —if it continues on to boil, the yogurt will curdle. Season to taste.

Caramelized butter is butter heated until it turns a nut-brown color. It's made by heating the butter and allowing the white mass that separates from the oil to caramelize.

Drizzle the butter over the soup, sprinkle with the rest of the dried mint, and serve.

CARAMEL CONSOMMÉ WITH SHIITAKE MUSHROOMS AND CRUNCHY VEGETABLES

Serves 6
Preparation time: 10 minutes
Cooking time: 5 minutes

1 Tbsp (15 mL) peanut oil
1 red onion, peeled and finely chopped
2 cloves garlic, peeled and finely chopped
1 thumb-sized piece fresh ginger, peeled and chopped
$^1/_4$ cup (50 mL) light soy sauce
$^1/_2$ cup (125 mL) soft light brown sugar
2 Tbsp Thai fish sauce (Nam Pla)
Grated rind of 2 limes
2 Tbsp (30 mL) lime juice, more if desired
3 cups (750 mL) hot water
$3^1/_2$ oz (100 g) fresh shiitake mushrooms, thinly sliced
1 handful snow peas or sugar snap peas
1 handful shelled peas
3 spring onions (scallions), cut in half lengthwise

Heat the oil in a skillet and lightly fry the onion and garlic without letting them brown.

Add the rest of the ingredients (except the water) and leave to cook for a few minutes.

Add enough hot water to dilute the sauce, and bring to a boil.

Throw the mushrooms and vegetables into the skillet and leave to cook for just a few minutes.

Serve in attractive bowls, accompanied by rice crackers.

PAN-FRIED FOIE GRAS WITH BALSAMIC CARAMEL AND RAW GOLD BALL TURNIPS

A CLASSIC DISH IN WHICH ROOT VEGETABLES UPSTAGE THE BALSAMIC CARAMEL. IN THIS VERSION, THE SLIGHTLY BITTER FLAVOR OF THE GOLD BALL TURNIPS, THINLY SLICED AND SERVED RAW, PROVIDES A DELICIOUS CONTRAST TO THE SMOOTHNESS OF THE FOIE GRAS AND THE SWEETNESS OF THE CARAMEL.

Serves 6

1/2 cup less 1 Tbsp (100 mL) granulated sugar
2 Tbsp (30 mL) water
1/4 cup (50 mL) balsamic vinegar
6 slices fresh foie gras, each about 3 1/2 oz (100 g)
   and 3/4 inch (2 cm) thick
Sea salt and freshly ground black pepper
2 Gold Ball turnips, washed, peeled if desired,
   and thinly sliced

Make a caramel with the sugar and water (see page 12). Remove from the heat, add the balsamic vinegar and stir well. Return the saucepan to the heat to dissolve any sugar crystals that may have formed. Keep to one side.

Pan-fry the slices of foie gras in a very hot skillet for no more than 1 minute, on each side.

Sprinkle with sea salt and pepper, drizzle with the caramel, and serve immediately, accompanied by the raw sliced turnips.

BAY SCALLOPS WITH VANILLA SAUCE AND BALSAMIC CARAMEL

THESE SMALL SCALLOPS MAKE A DELICIOUS ENTRÉE OR APPETIZER. COOKED WITH FRESH SEA SCALLOPS, THE LARGER COQUILLES SAINT-JACQUES, THEY ALSO MAKE A STYLISH MAIN COURSE.

Serves 4
Preparation time: 15 minutes
Cooking time: 10 minutes

1/2 cup less 1 Tbsp (100 mL) granulated sugar
2 Tbsp (30 mL) water
1/4 cup (50 mL) balsamic vinegar
2 Tbsp (30 mL) salted butter
1 shallot, peeled and finely chopped
3/4 lb (375 g) bay scallops (frozen will do but fresh
   are better)
3/4 cup (175 mL) whipping cream
1 vanilla bean, split in half lengthwise, seeds scraped
   out and set aside
Salt and freshly ground black pepper

Make a caramel with the sugar and water (see page 12). Remove from the heat, add the balsamic vinegar, and stir well. If sugar crystals form, dissolve them by returning the pan to the heat. Leave to cool.

Heat the butter in a skillet and sweat the shallot without allowing it to brown. Add the scallops and brown over a high heat. Remove the scallops and keep warm. Deglaze the skillet with the cream. Add only the seeds from the vanilla bean to the cream, stir well to disperse, and season to taste. (The empty bean can be put into a screw-top jar with sugar to make vanilla sugar.)

Serve the scallops in the vanilla sauce, trickling attractive shapes in the sauce with the balsamic caramel.

BLUEFIN TUNA TARTARE WITH RASPBERRY-VINEGAR CARAMEL

Serves 4
Preparation time: 25 minutes

For the caramel
1/2 cup less 1 Tbsp (100 mL) granulated sugar
2 Tbsp (30 mL) water
1/4 cup (50 mL) raspberry vinegar

For the tuna
3/4 lb (375 g) fresh bluefin tuna, cut in small cubes
2 Tbsp (30 mL) light soy sauce
2 shallots, peeled and finely chopped
White pepper

To serve
1 handful fresh raspberries
1 handful desiccated coconut, or freshly grated coconut

Make a caramel with the sugar and water (see page 12).

Remove from the heat, add the raspberry vinegar, and stir well. If sugar crystals form, dissolve them by returning the pan to the heat. Leave the caramel to cool completely.

Mix the diced tuna with the soy sauce and shallots, and season with pepper. Use a small flan ring or cookie cutter to form a tuna round in the center of each serving dish.

To serve, drizzle a little caramel over the tuna rounds, and decorate with a few raspberries and a little coconut.

domestically disabled

CIABATTA STEAK SANDWICH WITH CARAMELIZED ONIONS

Use caramelized onions to add flavor to burgers and sandwiches. Here, the usual "plastic" bread has been replaced with a delicious ciabatta. Individual ready-to-bake ciabattas are now widely available, and are ideal for hot meat sandwiches.

PIZZA WITH CARAMELIZED ONIONS, EGGPLANT, ANCHOVIES, AND MOZZARELLA CHEESE

Serves 6
Preparation time: 25 minutes
Cooking time: 10 minutes

$\frac{1}{4}$ cup (50 mL) butter
3 large onions, peeled and thinly sliced
1–2 tsp (5–10 mL) granulated sugar (optional)
2–3 Tbsp (30–45 mL) olive oil
$\frac{1}{2}$ eggplant, rinsed and cut in strips
1 ready-made pizza base
3$\frac{1}{2}$ oz (100 g) mozzarella cheese (preferably made
   with buffalo's milk), drained and diced
3–4 anchovies in oil, chopped

Preheat the oven to 400°F (200°C).

Heat the butter in a skillet and, when it begins to bubble, add the onions.

Cook over moderate heat for about 10 minutes, stirring frequently so that they become soft and caramelized. Add a little sugar if you want a more pronounced caramel flavor. Keep to one side.

Heat the olive oil in a skillet and fry the eggplant strips until they are nicely browned.

Lay the pizza base on a baking sheet. Spread the onions on the pizza base, alternate the mozzarella cheese and eggplant, and sprinkle with anchovies.

Bake in the oven for about 10 minutes and serve piping hot.

CARAMELIZED ONION AND FETA CHEESE TARTLETS

A winning combination that will use up any leftover onions from the pizza recipe (see this page).

If making from scratch, prepare the onions as for the pizza. Put $\frac{1}{2}$ Tbsp onions in each ready-made tartlet and top with a small piece of feta.

CAMEMBERT WITH CARAMEL

AN ATTRACTIVE AND PRACTICAL WAY TO ADD PIZAZZ TO A CHEESE BOARD
OR LIVEN UP A DESSERT. NOT EASY TO CUT, HOWEVER, AND WATCH OUT FOR
THOSE CROWNS AND FILLINGS!

Serves 6
Preparation time: 10 minutes

For the caramel
½ cup less 1 Tbsp (100 mL) granulated sugar
2 Tbsp water

For the camembert
1 best-quality, mature camembert
Dried fruit, pecan nuts, peanuts, raisins, figs, plums, etc.

Make a caramel with the sugar and water (see page 12).

Arrange the dried fruit and nuts on the camembert and drizzle with the warm
caramel, allowing it to run down the sides. Leave to cool and harden.

INDEX OF RECIPES

ADDRESSES

ALESSI
31, rue Boissy d'Anglas
75008 Paris
00 33 (0) 1 42 66 31 00

ASIATIDES
www.asiatides.com

B.V.T.
04 90 38 00 81

BÔ
8, rue Saint-Merri
75004 Paris
00 33 (0) 1 42 72 84 64

THE CONRAN SHOP
117, rue du Bac
75007 Paris
00 33 (0) 1 42 84 10 01

ELITIS
35, rue de Bellechasse
75007 Paris
00 33 (0) 1 45 51 51 00

HABITAT
0 800 010 800

HOME AUTOUR DU MONDE
8, rue des Francs-Bourgeois
75004 Paris
00 33 (0) 1 42 77 06 08

MAISON DE VACANCES
63-64, galerie Montpensier
75001 Paris
00 33 (0) 1 47 03 99 74

QUARTZ
12, rue des Quatre-Vents
75006 Paris
00 33 (0) 1 43 54 03 00

IKEA
0 825 826 826

SENTOU
29, rue François Miron
75004 Paris
00 33 (0) 1 42 78 50 60

FINE FOOD

LADURÉE
21 rue Bonaparte
75006 Paris
75, avenue des Champs Elysées
75008 Paris
16, rue Royale
75008 Paris
62, boulevard Haussmann
Le Printemps du luxe
75009 Paris

PÂTISSERIE JOËL DURAND
3 boulevard Victor Hugo
13210 Saint Remy de Provence

THE BERKELEY
Wilton Place
Knightsbridge
London SW1X 7RL
Telephone: +44 (0)20 7235 6000
Fax: +44 (0)20 7235 4330
Email: info@the-berkeley.co.uk

ACCESSORIES

ALESSI
Saucepans and skillets, pages: 5, 10, 124. Plate, page: 130.

ASIATIDES
Bowls, pages: 46, 76. Lunch box, page: 56. Glass, page: 74. Spoon, page: 142.

BÔ
Glass, page: 24. Wooden boards, pages: 90, 128. Spoon, page: 120.

ELITIS
Textiles, pages: 5, 50.

HABITAT
Dessert glasses, pages: 70, 72. Bowl, page: 142. Platter, page: 133.

HOME AUTOUR DU MONDE
Bowls, page: 24.

IKEA
Cake stand, page: 96. Dishes, pages: 118, 138. Ramekins, pages: 108, 109.

MAISON DE VACANCES
Textiles and skins, pages: 8, 32, 38, 66, 117, 127, 150. Feathery cushion, page: 92.

QUARTZ
Glass dish, page: 38. Plates, pages: 62, 99, 140.

SENTOU
Spoons, pages: 24, 44, 147. Trays, pages: 36, 117, 132. Dishes and plates], pages: 60, 70, 98, 102, 122, 146, 148.

THE CONRAN SHOP
Glasses, pages: 68, 69. Sauceboat, page: 80. Chopping boards, pages: 106, 134. Plates, page: 136.

© Marabout – Hachette Livre, 2005

All rights reserved. No part of this publication may be reproduced in any form or by any means, photocopying, digitization, microfilm, or otherwise, without the prior written permission of the copyright owners.

Published in the United States and Canada in 2006 by Whitecap Books Ltd.

For more information, contact Whitecap Books Ltd., 351 Lynn Avenue, North Vancouver, British Columbia, Canada V7J 2C4. Visit our website at www.whitecap.ca.

ACKNOWLEDGMENTS
La maison Ladurée,
Paula Fitzherbert and the charming staff at The Berkeley
Greg, Lou, Mahmoud, Denise, Martine, Odile B, and Max.
Ivan Mulcahy, smoother than caramel but not as sweet.
Accessories: Emmanuelle Javelle

ISBN 1-55285-815-4
ISBN 978-1-55285-815-8

Printed in Singapore